I NEVER LEARNED TO DOUBT

LESSONS I'VE LEARNED

about

THE DANGERS OF DOUBT

and

THE FREEDOM OF FAITH

I NEVER LEARNED TO DOUBT

**LESSONS I'VE LEARNED ABOUT
THE DANGERS OF DOUBT AND THE FREEDOM OF FAITH**

Jesse Duplantis

JESSE DUPLANTIS MINISTRIES
Destrehan, LA

Published by Jesse Duplantis
PO Box 1089
Destrehan, LA 70047
www.jdm.org

ISBN 13: 978-1-6341-6735-2

Printed in the USA

1 2 3 4 5 6 7 | 25 24 23 22 21

CONTENTS

"You Asked to See Me. Turn Around."

WHAT I LEARNED BY GETTING WHAT I COULDN'T HANDLE

I was a baby Christian and hadn't been saved long when I started noticing how many times God physically revealed Himself to people in the Bible. I was really amazed at the idea and started to think about what it might be like to have an experience like that. Now, I was naive. When it came to the things of God, I didn't have much experience . . . or spiritual sense. As a baby Christian, you could say I still had on my spiritual "diapers," and I became preoccupied with the idea of seeing God for myself.

I read the Word of God every chance that I got and I was learning. While I didn't have much wisdom yet, what I did have was what all babies have—a sense of awe and wonder when it came to the things of God. I still have that today. Like all "babies" in the Lord, back then, I thought I could convince God to visit me if I just laid out what He'd already done for others. So, I began to talk to God like that all the time when I prayed. I just plain wanted to see something with my own eyes.

I said, "Now, God, You showed Yourself to men like Adam, Abraham, Noah, Moses, Peter, and Paul. Why won't You show Yourself to me? What's wrong? I'm just a Cajun from South Louisiana, but I would like to see You. You said You're no respecter of persons, but it looks like You are." I actually didn't doubt God could do it . . . but I *was* trying to twist His arm and convince Him to show Himself to me. Like I said, I was still a baby Christian, and I didn't have much sense spiritually—but God loves babies and, of course, He understood all of that. God sees beyond our ignorance about Him and looks at our heart.

I often talked to Him about visiting me. I just wanted to touch Him in a deeper way and to be closer—and I thought that if I could just see Him for myself, I'd have more faith. Although I was thinking and praying wrongly when it came to faith, God heard me. And He didn't just *hear* me, but He answered me, too.

Now, I've never been one of those believers who is always searching for a preacher to talk to God for me or tell me what God said about me. I believed in prophecy and knew it was valuable, but I knew that it wasn't as valuable for everyday life as the scriptures. I also knew from my own experience and the Word that I could talk to the Lord directly, and He could communicate with my spirit directly, too. Still, when someone calls you out of a pew to tell you something God said He's going to do concerning *you*, well, your ears perk allllll the way up!

The Prophecy, the Anticipation, and the Exhaustion

My wife, Cathy, and I went to a church meeting one night. We were just sitting there listening to the preacher speak when, suddenly, he just stopped talking. He was silent for a little while and then looked right in our direction. Then, he pointed at me. "You, sir . . . come up here," he said. He wanted me to get out of my seat and go to the altar where he was standing.

My first thought was, *Oh, God, what did I do wrong?* I really didn't think I'd done anything wrong, but being singled out sometimes can feel that way. I went up to the front like he asked, and he looked me dead in the eye.

"I don't know who you are, sir," he said to me in front of everyone, "but the Lord tells me that you have been asking to see Him." Let me tell you, my antennae went all the way up after hearing that!

He said, "The Lord told me to tell you that He shall grant you a visitation." My jaw just about hit the floor. He paused and then continued.

"He's coming to see you. He shall come to you at night," the preacher said. "You shall be in bed with your wife. She will be sleeping. She will not hear and will not wake up. But the Lord *will* come to see you."

I looked him in the eye and asked him directly, "When?"

He said, "Quickly." And that was that. He sent me back to my seat. Well, my mind was racing. I couldn't wait for the preacher to finish speaking so I could just go home and go to bed! I thought, *This minister is a true man of God.*

You see, I hadn't told *anybody* that I'd been talking to God about visiting me, not even my wife. I went home thinking the visitation would happen that very night. So, that night, Cathy went on to bed like she usually did and instead of staying up later like I usually did, I went to bed at the same time as her. I wanted to sleep, but I couldn't close my eyes to save my life! I was too excited, so I decided that if I just stayed awake, I wouldn't miss out. So, that's what I did. I was flat determined to stay AWAKE.

I was looking around everywhere in that little bedroom. I didn't sleep at all that night. I waited up all night for God to visit, but nothing happened. *Nothing.* God didn't come. I was disappointed. So, I tried to stay up the next night, and the next night too. For three or four nights in a row, I can't remember which, I did my best to fight off sleep. If I nodded off, I wouldn't be down for long because I'd jerk myself back up. Night after night, I tried to stay awake and night after night, nothing happened. I became exhausted. I couldn't do it anymore, and I started just letting myself sleep easy again.

Two weeks passed of sleeping through the night and every morning I woke up disappointed. I started to get irritated. As a baby Christian, I had less than zero patience. One morning, I had a short little pity-party for one, and I thought, *Man, maybe that guy missed it . . . maybe God doesn't want to come and see me at all!*

I knew that God could do what He wanted. I knew that I wasn't promised in the Word of God that He would visit me, or anybody. I knew that all I had was my desire and that preacher's words, and I knew that if God was going to come see me, it was going to have to be a sovereign act. In other words, He had to *want* to do that for some reason. I started to think maybe the preacher wasn't talking to me prophetically after all, and that maybe he'd just happened to hit on my desire by coincidence.

I was wrong.

The Wind, the Power, and the Voice

That very night I went to bed like I usually do, a little later than Cathy. She was already fast asleep when I turned onto my stomach. I prayed like I normally do, thanking God for the day, and then I fell off to sleep.

All of a sudden in the middle of the night, I woke up and I wasn't groggy—I went from being fully asleep to being wide-awake. That alone was strange to me. I looked over at the clock on the nightstand beside me and saw it was three o'clock in the morning. I could feel that *something* was so different in that room, I can't explain it, and for some reason I didn't even think about God or the prophecy I'd received. I was just in the moment, as they say, and that's when I noticed a light wind beginning to blow on me.

At first, I thought it was the air-conditioning unit in the window, but then the wind got stronger . . . and stronger, and stronger. It didn't register yet what was happening to me. I always sleep sort of between my side and my stomach, on that angle, with one foot off the bed and my arm around my pillow. So, I remained like that, looking sideways feeling the wind, and from my position, I could see our window—and that sight just blew me away. The curtains weren't just blowing a little from the wind, but they were blowing hard and flying up above the rods. They were straight up! That's when I knew that I was experiencing something supernatural.

The wind in that bedroom was so strong and so strange, I've never felt anything like it before—I can hardly describe this wind because it just wasn't normal. Being from South Louisiana, I've been in hurricanes and felt wind before. But this wind didn't just hit my body; I could feel it blowing *through* my body. It was going through my eyes. It was going through and through and under my fingernails. I could feel it pushing through my skin, like it was blowing through my pores into my body. It is so hard to describe.

As this wind blew, I felt my body start losing its strength. Even though I wasn't moving at all and still stayed in the same position on my stomach holding my pillow with my head sideways, I kept feeling weaker and weaker—and soon, I felt like I was being pinned to the bed. I knew if I tried, I *could* move and turn my body the other way to see who/what the wind was coming from on the opposite side of the room, and yet I felt like I couldn't. I don't know if that makes any sense, but that's how I felt. It was wild and I don't care if anybody believes me or not. Man, this is what was going on and I will never forget it as long as I live.

What's happening? I thought to myself. And just as I had that thought, I heard a Voice speaking audibly in that room through the wind.

The Voice said, "You asked to see Me. Turn around."

It shook me to my core. I suddenly didn't think about that wind or how my body felt under the pressure of it because I realized that this was the visitation . . . and the presence of God was in that little room.

"GOD!" I cried out, still lying in the same position.

He said it again, "You asked to see Me. Turn around."

I didn't want to turn around—I was afraid and I didn't know what to do. I felt as if my flesh was jumping off my bones. It was such an intense physical pressure, and it was like my body couldn't handle it. I thought I couldn't handle turning around because I'd face that intense pressure even more, so I didn't move. I was locked into place by my own fearful mind.

I heard the Voice again for the third and final time, "You asked to see Me. Turn around."

I wouldn't do it . . . but I suddenly had a thought. *Cathy would look. She'll do it!* So, because I was facing my nightstand and she was asleep behind me, I used one arm to reach back and I nudged her with my elbow.

"Cathy! Wake up!!" I said and pushed my elbow into her again, "Don't you know God's in the room?!" I wanted help! I needed her to get up and be with me in the situation. So, I used my elbow again and again, but the woman just *wouldn't* wake up.

Just then, I realized that the prophecy I had received weeks ago was coming to pass exactly the way the preacher had said it. I thought,

God is in the room! With the wind still blowing and my mind racing, I gave up. Knowing that I would not turn around to face Him, I cried out for mercy.

"God, forgive me for being so stupid!" I yelled into the wind, "Forgive me! I prayed wrong!"

Immediately, the wind stopped. The curtains stopped flying up to the ceiling and fell back into their normal place. When I saw them drop, I turned around as fast as I could and finally looked . . . and that's when I saw NOTHING. That was the moment I knew I had just blown my chance. The regret and frustration at myself swelled up in me. I got so mad that I just started berating myself aloud.

I was out of breath before I even started griping at myself for some reason, but that didn't stop me! I started talking to myself saying, "You stupid idiot! What's the matter with you?! You asked to see God. Then, when He comes to see you, you don't even turn around? What's the matter with you? Idiot!" Then, acting more like an idiot, I started to get mad at Cathy, too.

I couldn't believe that my wife could sleep through the wind in that room much less the Voice. I knew I'd nudged her so hard it would have woken up an elephant, so how could I not wake up a 105 pound woman? I was ticked off.

In the quiet of that room and the heat of my own frustration, I elbowed her again to try to wake her up. This time, guess what? She woke up! I couldn't believe it. She turned to me half asleep and said, "What's the matter?"

"You just missed it!" I griped.

"What?" she asked.

"God was here in this very room, but you haaaaad to sleep," I said, and got even more mad, "So just go back to sleep!"

I know I was wrong, but I was so frustrated at myself and was just looking to blame somebody else, too. Cathy wasn't even fazed. She just looked at me, still half asleep, and asked the question I didn't want to answer.

"What did He look like?" she said.

I huffed and puffed, embarrassed, and then just said it.

"I . . . I . . . I didn't turn around!!!"

The Regret, the Lesson, and the Choice to Grow

I got out of bed and headed toward the living room. I was angry with myself, but weak and tired feeling, and the experience had made me hungry too. So, I went to the living room by way of the refrigerator and made myself a sandwich. As I sat down on the couch eating it, I just kept feeling like an idiot. I had so much regret, and my mind wouldn't stop beating me up. I was so disappointed in myself and so, like I always do when I'm troubled, I just started talking aloud to God about it.

I said, "God, You came to me. I heard You with my physical ears, and I didn't even turn around!"

I heard His familiar Voice in my spirit speak this, "I'm glad you didn't. It's better that you not see Me and still believe."

"But it's my heart's desire to see You," I said.

He told me, "But you wouldn't be able to handle my glory. You're living in a corruptible vessel, a body that will die."

"Is that why I was hurting?" I asked.

"That's why your flesh was hurting. Your flesh cannot handle the glory of Who I Am," He said.

I stopped talking. I sat and ate my sandwich in the living room, just going over all that just happened. I realized then that I knew what God's voice really sounded like in my own ears, and not just in my spirit . . . and yet I was processing the idea that He was "glad" I hadn't turned around because it was "better" to Him that I *believed without seeing*. That is a lesson that bred a greater desire in me to pursue even more faith than I already had.

This is a true story that happened to me. I don't care if people believe it or not because I know what happened to me—but in all the encounters with the supernatural I've had over my many years, I can tell you that not one built my faith. I'm blessed to have had quite a few unusual supernatural experiences in my many years of serving the Lord, but this particular one was so important for me. It showed me that I didn't have the faith or understanding I needed yet to receive what I had asked for from God. I needed to grow in faith to meet the challenge of living for God and receiving, too.

"I didn't turn around" became a lesson for me, and the lesson is this: Sometimes, we can ask God for something that we can't yet receive. It shines a light on our weakness to handle what He delivers—and the most important thing He gives us is Himself. It takes faith to receive salvation. It takes faith to receive healing. It takes faith to do anything God asks in His Word in order to receive from Him. It's not faith to receive first and then believe. Our growth isn't ever going to come by just receiving from God—we draw close to Him first, we read His Word first, and we grow as we apply it. Then, we receive. It's how faith works.

Sometimes, we just need to grow . . . and God will give us the opportunity by giving us what we can't handle to show us the limitations of our earthly nature in light of His divine limitlessness. So, again, we can ask for what we can't handle, and if God chooses to give it to us *before* we can handle it, He is just using the experience to show us where we need to grow spiritually. He's stimulating us to go further with Him. Our growth as believers is always going to be linked to two things: wisdom and faith.

Wisdom isn't knowledge. You can know a lot and still have no wisdom. The Word says that the beginning of wisdom is the fear of the Lord—and this was never more true to me than at the moment when I could not turn around. You see, I was a baby Christian with passion and fire in my heart. I was pure-hearted in my desire to see the Lord. And yet I didn't understand what I was asking for, and I didn't know that I couldn't handle it until I was confronted with God's presence. I would come to be able to handle so much more of God as I grew in faith. I've found that in all my years as a believer, my growth never came by what I could *see*, no matter how spectacular the sight was—it always came by what I learned in the Word and what I had the guts to *believe*.

I knew I could turn around, but I wouldn't turn around. Fear for my own body's safety kept me in place. I felt scared when confronted with the power of His glory. And although I knew I'd asked God to do something grand for me—to visit me—I found out that, in the heat of it, I wanted to hold onto my own flesh more than I wanted to experience something divine. God knew this, but I didn't. I believe He came *knowing* that I would not turn around, and yet He still came anyway. What a blessing it is when you get what you ask for . . . and realize you need to grow to handle it. Many people only want the successes, but it's in our weakness that He is made strong in us.

I have no idea what I would have seen if I'd turned around that day or if I would have even made it out alive if I had. I just don't know. But I do know that the reality of our God is so much more than we can take in mentally and physically—and that it is *better*, as He said, to believe without seeing. That is what this book is all about.

Doubt didn't keep me fixed to my bed that night, but fear did. They don't always go hand in hand, although sometimes they do. I know that God works in our spirit because that's the only place we can handle it, and our body itself is not strong enough to face God. So, our goal should be to become spiritually aware, strong, and humble before God as we live this life—and faith is the key to all of that. Because if you can't believe that God can do something or fulfill His Word, how can you ever receive Who He is or what He says? You can't.

Childlike faith is what Jesus preached. It's not *childish* faith or what some call "blind" faith. To me, it is an eyes-wide-open wonder and a pure acceptance of God, and of pure belief that "what God said, He can do"—even if we have to grow to meet the challenge of receiving what we ask of Him.

The Humility, the Conversation, and the Openness to the Call

I was humbled by that experience as a baby Christian and awed by it, too. I wanted to tell someone that I trusted, who might be able to guide me. I spoke to my pastor about the experience, but he didn't really understand it. So, I talked to another man who I esteemed highly in the faith, and his words confirmed what I already knew but didn't want to accept.

This man was a minister, too. He was older, and a precious man of God that I considered to be the epitome of dignity. He had been ministering for 50 years and, now that I think about it, was about as old as I am today at the time of the writing of this book. I knew he was anointed—he had a track record of wisdom I admired—and I hoped that he would believe what had happened to me.

After telling him about my experience, I said, "This really happened to me. What do you think? Why did it happen?" I wanted help grasping it because, like all babies, I was looking to someone older to help me understand things. I didn't want him to think I was crazy, but I could tell by his eyes at the end of me sharing the experience that he believed me—and that's when I saw that he began to tear up and cry. Something in the story touched him, and also revealed something to him about my future. He couldn't answer the questions I had, but he gave me the confirmation I needed—and he also gave me a word I didn't want to hear.

"I don't know why it happened, but I know it's of the Lord," he said, and then he paused and told me, "You're called to the ministry." Now, I knew in the back of my heart that God was pulling on me for that, though I also somehow knew it wasn't the time for it—I just knew He would one day ask me. It was like He had been giving me hints of it in my spirit, and each time I'd always push those things away.

"You're called to the ministry" is not what I wanted to hear or what I was looking for at all. I'd been a rock musician before I got saved, and I thought that talking was not my gift. My gift was music. I had no desire to preach to anyone. So, I said, "No, you don't understand. I can play music, but I'm not a minister."

He said, "Well, that's what God is calling you to do. Because you aren't already one, He doesn't have to un-train you. He can just train you now." We talked some more and I left with peace. Even though I wasn't interested in being in the ministry at all, I began being more open.

Like I said, I didn't have more faith because of the experience, and I had more growing to do, but I knew from the Word of God that it would only come one way. The Romans 10:17 way, which is all about hearing: *"So then faith cometh by hearing, and hearing by the Word of God."* Notice it doesn't say it comes by supernatural experiences. Our ears must be involved to grow in faith, and not only our physical ears but also the "hearing" of our heart.

In other words, what will we "hear" or *receive* into our heart through understanding? Jesus shined a light on this type of "hearing" in Matthew 11:15 when He said, *"He that hath ears to hear, let him hear.*" Everybody that day heard Him with their physical ears, but He wanted them to "hear" with their heart and understand the truth of what He was saying that day.

The Most Important Growth-Practice for Me

Facing truth often means we have to put away our preconceived ideas—it takes guts to do that, and humility. God's ways are higher than ours, and our faith is in Him and not our own intellect. Wisdom is the principle thing, and it isn't at its highest when we only put faith in the wisdom of men. The Word is so valuable to me, and I've chosen to make it the meditation of my heart—which is how *"hearing, and hearing by the Word of God"* can happen. I read the Word, study it, and listen to messages about it. But the most important thing that I do is make the scriptures the *meditation* of my heart like Psalm 19:14 tells me to do. This means I yield myself to God by giving attention to His Word in my own mind—I rehearse the scriptures to myself. I think on them and ponder them. I speak them aloud to myself every day, too. Do doubtful thoughts come up? Sure, but I cast down thoughts that try to exalt themselves above what God says. I choose to "doubt the doubt." God's Word is living, and it changes me from the inside out as I meditate on it—letting its truth turn over in my mind and realizing how it applies to me has changed my life.

The things we say over and over to ourselves matter. If we want to grow in faith, then those things we say to ourselves over and over need to be faith-based—they need to be the scripture and the principles behind those scriptures, too. To grow in faith, the focus must be on the wisdom of God as it relates to us and this world, and not just random thoughts about what's happening or not happening. We can't even face or deal with "what's happening" with wisdom if we don't think about it through the lens of the Word—because God is the holder of ultimate wisdom, and there is no greater wisdom than whatever He says. It takes humility to accept that.

I began to grow in greater faith as I immersed my mind and my heart in wisdom, as I continued *"hearing, and hearing by the Word of God."* And I also changed the way I had been praying, too. I stopped saying, "I want to see You, God" and instead, I began saying things like, "God, I don't need to see You to believe You" when I prayed. I talked to God within my spirit all the time. I knew He heard me whether He said anything or not. I knew it was better to believe, and so believing itself became the greatest focus in growth.

I also started to question how many other things I may have been praying wrongly! I realized how merciful God is with His babies, too. He knew I was growing in Him and that I just wanted more of Him. He knew that I wasn't interested in anything but hearing what He had to say. So, I kept studying His Word more and more, to learn and get to know not only Him, but also His *ways*. The more Word you get inside of you, the more you start to expand your mind about how God works.

God *Put* Me Into the Ministry

One thing I must say here: God doesn't put spiritual babies on the field. I want you to know that I didn't immediately go into the ministry just because I felt a nudge or because a minister confirmed it. I just immersed myself in the Word and volunteered at my church, doing what I knew to do—leading music and building the choir. I still didn't want to go into the ministry, and since God didn't ask me directly yet, I just kept focusing on growing in Him and doing what I could to help my local community church. I really thought God might forget it and let me off the hook! Like I said, I never wanted to be a preacher, and yet . . . here I am!

I just wanted to attend church like everybody else, but that's not what God had in store for me. I can honestly say that, like the apostle Paul, God *put* me into the ministry. That's a story for another time, but let me just say that He did ask me directly. Finally, I broke down and answered His call to ministry—I accepted what I didn't want because I knew that what He wanted was more important.

In my first year of ministry, I held 51 weeks of meetings. I was so busy, I felt like I was preaching constantly. I never called and asked anyone if I could preach at their church. It began in 1978 when, out of the blue, a pastor asked me to speak to their church youth group—I accepted, told my testimony, and from that one meeting I got seven invitations. You see, God set me up! In that youth service, there were seven pastors present—and they talked to me after the service and invited me to their churches. I booked meetings with them and from those, word got around and other pastors asked me to preach at their churches, too. Before I knew it, the first year of ministry was completely booked up, and from that time until today, it just hasn't stopped.

The Word Renews the Mind, but Faith Changes the Heart— It's Not a Mindset, It's a Heart Reset

I've learned that it doesn't matter what other people say if they don't say what God says! If God says something, it's going to happen. I've heard many people say, "I won't believe it until I see it" and even if they do "see it," they'll respond, "I see it, but I don't believe it! I can't believe my own eyes!" Human beings are fickle like that—but there is a stability that I've found in faith that just can't match the human mind's fickleness.

The Word renews the mind, but faith in the Word changes the heart. You see, you can't convince your mind of something your heart refuses to believe or accept. You can say "I want to be blessed financially" all day long, but if deep in your heart you believe you can't really experience financial success, then your heart will win that battle. That's why faith needs to get into your heart. It's why faith isn't just about a mindset—it's about a heart reset!

Jesus said, *"Blessed are the pure in heart: for they shall see God"* (Matthew 5:8). All of us who believe will one day "see God" in Heaven, but this verse also shows us the importance of purity in the heart itself. You are blessed when you are pure of heart. It's easy to *see* the effect of God and His principles in this life when you are pure of heart, and I believe that it takes faith to become pure of heart.

I love the portion of the Our Father prayer that Jesus prayed where He instructed us to pray that, *"Thy kingdom come, Thy will be done in earth, as it is in heaven"* (Matthew 6:10). A pure-of-heart person will read that and just accept that God's will *can* be done right here on the earth as it is in Heaven—because they don't doubt that God can do anything! Doubt is sneaky. In this book, I hope to inspire you to start living without doubt when it comes to the things of God—because He is real, powerful, and more than able to help you experience a life like you've never imagined.

Faith is freeing. In this book, I share some of my own experiences as a believer and also teach on the dangers of doubt and the power of faith that I hope will inspire you to think differently and start living with more freedom. We serve a supernatural God. He's not religious, but He is pure—and so powerful that one day He's going to change the whole world in an instant. One day, every knee will bow and every tongue will confess Him as Lord. There will not be a soul that does not recognize His power and authority. Why wait to do that when you can do it today? May you be inspired as you read to let go of whatever has been keeping you back from saying, "I don't have to see You, God . . . I choose to humble myself before You and simply BELIEVE."

If God Could Change *Me*, I Knew He Could Do Anything

I REFUSE TO DOUBT THE GOD WHO ALWAYS BELIEVES IN ME

I grew up in a dysfunctional family, and I learned early that you couldn't trust most people. My childhood was marked by poverty and disappointment in people. I was consistently told what I couldn't do because I was "nothing but a Cajun" and "we can't do that." I rejected that inside of my heart, but it did affect my mind—but God gave me a new mind, the mind of Christ, when I found Him!

Jesus had the same problem when He went into ministry. In His hometown, people sneered at Him, asking, "Isn't this Mary's boy? He's nothing but a carpenter!" That's my paraphrase, but that's essentially what they were saying. The Word says in Mark 6:36 that He could do no mighty work there, except healing a few sick folk, because of their unbelief. Now, think about this: If *Jesus* Himself was thought of as incapable of doing great things to some people, how much more will *you* be thought of as incapable of doing great things by some people?

We can't be swayed by the words of people who judge us by what they think of themselves. The Word helps us to bust out of that mentality that others try to inflict upon us. We must realize that every time we accept or agree with *whatever* doesn't line up with what God said about us, we are hindering our own progress in life.

A lot of people who make it out of poverty do so because they didn't allow the poverty to get inside of them. They may have lived in a low-income housing project, but the "low-income" mentality of the housing project didn't get *inside* of them. They may have been told they weren't worthy, but the unworthy mentality didn't get inside of them. Something else rose up and that something was the real them! That's what God wants to do with us. Even if we come to Him with no knowledge, He will help us to gain insight about our worth and wisdom about life.

Even with No Concept of God, God Can Step in and Change Everything

I was born in 1949. My parents were poor Cajun French people, and I was born in Algiers, Louisiana on the point overlooking the Mississippi River across from New Orleans. My father worked in the oil field, like so many Cajun men still do today.

As you may have heard me say before in my sermons, my family wasn't religious until my dad received a miraculous healing of his eyesight after being blinded during an accident with acid on an oil production platform. I was just a boy when he came home blinded, locked himself into his bedroom, and began to cry out to God for help. "God, if You heal me, I'll raise my kids to serve You!" he told me he said to God at one point.

Daddy was a manual laborer, and so no eyesight meant no money. When he locked himself in the bedroom, he was breaking down emotionally and mentally because he knew he wouldn't be able to work and support his family without eyesight. While he had no real concept of God, He knew that God was God, and He could do anything. Sure, he was trying to bargain with God—but, again, God can see through some of our wrong prayers even—and in that bedroom, Daddy exercised more than just emotions. He exercised pure-hearted faith in God.

God calls Himself the Alpha and Omega, the beginning and the end. Jesus is called the Author and Finisher of our faith. When we are sincere and have faith, it's amazing what we can receive from God, even if we don't know very much. I believe Daddy had faith in that moment, and not just sadness or emotion about his accident— he reached out to God and the results didn't just change the course of his life, but it changed the course of mine, too.

When Daddy woke up the next day after praying loudly to God and crying himself to sleep, he could *see*. It was a miracle and he knew in his heart that God had heard his prayer. After that, we were at church every time the doors opened. Daddy made good on his promise, whether we liked it or not—and I did not like it! I hated church and we went to a bunch of them. Through the years of my childhood, my parents roamed from church to church trying to find their way closer to God.

For years, when I was a kid, when somebody asked me what church I went to, I'd say, "Pick one, I've been there!" It was culture shock to go from Catholic, to Baptist, to Church of God, Church of Christ, Assembly of God, and every other one in our area. We ended up in a Pentecostal one too, and that is when it all got even more "religious" and full of hard rules. I went because I had to, but I didn't believe much at all. I blew a lot of it off because it just didn't matter to me.

When I was a kid, I didn't think much about God. I was focused on the outside world way more than any "God stuff," as I called it. I was creative. I played the guitar, the bass, the piano, and just about anything else I picked up. My dad taught me a couple chords on the guitar so I could help play songs at the church, and I found I had an ear for music.

I was focused and practical, and since we grew up dirt poor, I saw firsthand the misery poverty brought and I wanted out of it. Like I said, I never thought much about God. I thought about what I could see with my own eyes, touch with my own hands, and do for myself. It wasn't that I didn't believe in God . . . it's just that I thought He was irrelevant to my own life.

You see, although my parents found God, they didn't get the teaching they needed on how to think higher of themselves or their children. They found themselves in a church with people who loved God but believed that He was about to hit them with a lightning bolt every time they did wrong.

Unworthiness was preached more than love or anything else. So, my mom and daddy passed on all the "can'ts" they heard all their lives to me because that's what they believed inside. Poverty had gotten inside of them. Unworthiness had gotten inside of them. Feeling like nothing had gotten inside of them. What else could they pass on then, except all that junk? As a result, I didn't want anything to do with God. I figured I could do better on my own, and that if nobody believed in me, I'd have to believe in myself.

A Success and a Mess—and Still not Happy

When God came into my life, I'd already made both a success and a mess of my life. I was 24 years old. I'd gotten to a place where I had always wanted to be—playing music and earning more money than I had imagined I could earn as a kid. I had all the money and freedom that I wanted. I did what I wanted, when I wanted, and how I wanted, and I just didn't care if anybody liked it or not.

I was a typical rock musician in the 1970s, and that means, outside of furthering my musical career, I lived doing drugs and drinking too much. I drank a bottle of whisky just as my "regular drinking"—and then I started my fun drinking later. While none of it ever impeded me from playing music or making money, I had come to a place in my life where I was angry and hard inside.

Everything I'd dreamed of doing, I'd already done and I was flat shocked that none of it made me feel really happy or at peace. I had fun temporarily, but I was miserable deep inside. In fact, I didn't even realize how miserable I was until God came into my life. It's amazing how just a little light can show you how dark things have gotten. Well, when I made Jesus my Lord, I didn't get "just a little light"—it was like a floodlight came in and nothing, I mean absolutely nothing, looked or felt the same to me. The purity of God's effect on me shined a bright light on every bit of filth around me in the music scene.

Second Corinthians 5:17 talks about what happens when a person finds God through Jesus Christ—when they are suddenly not only living for themselves but are living "in Christ"—and that verse perfectly described me back then, and it still describes me today. *"Therefore if any man be in Christ, he is a new creature: old things are passed away; behold, all things are become new."*

I like the words "passed away" because that means dead! Old things became dead to me. I became a "new creature"—meaning something different than I ever was before, and something different than anybody I was raised with in the church as a kid. The word "behold" in that verse means "look," and I can say that everybody who knew me could see that I was different. Something had changed IN me and it affected everything about me. What happened? JESUS happened, and the freedom that came with knowing Him. And after that, ALL things became new for me.

From the moment I stepped out of that hotel bathroom in Boston, Massachusetts, where I invited Jesus into my heart after watching Billy Graham talk about the love of God on television, I was new and I knew it. I was changed. I had heard a message that cracked my hardened heart, and I sure didn't want my wife to see that, or my daughter—so I snuck into that hotel bathroom just to be alone, to get away, and to talk honestly to God. I told Him I didn't know if He was real, but if He was real, to come into my life and change me. I invited Him in and that day, on Labor Day weekend in 1974, He came and He saved my life.

From that day forward, I began to cut a new path in life . . . one without DOUBT. I wasn't going to stay in the sin-sick world of my music career. I wasn't going back to the religion of my childhood either. I was going somewhere totally new.

I Have *Chosen* Not to Doubt God— Why Would I Doubt the One Who Believed in Me So Much?

Choices are important—and I've chosen not to doubt God. I've chosen to take every opportunity to just believe. I decided way back then that if God could change *me*, He could do anything!

When I began preaching, every preacher I'd ever heard preached that poverty was holy. It was such an entrenched doctrine that every believer I knew thought it was true. "Poverty is holy" is a lie that is still being preached today, regardless of the fact that God is holy and Heaven is by no means a place of poverty. If poverty were holy, God would be poor in every way, but He's not—He is abundant in every way. Even materially, the Word lets us know that Heaven is filled with things like mansions, foundations of precious stone, and golden streets. That's a whole other book, but suffice it to say that even though I heard lots of people tell me poverty was holy, I found out for myself in the Word that it's just not true. So, what did I do? I chose to believe the Word, and guess what? In over 40 years of ministry, I've never had a financial deficit. I've never had to lay anybody off because I didn't have enough to pay them either. I may have started small, but God didn't limit me to staying small. I found in His Word that I would only be limited by my own faith—and so I decided to take the limits off of my thinking and stop listening to people whose only goal was to tell me what I "couldn't" do.

I've always been an all or nothing kind of person—if I'm going to do something, I'm not interested in going halfway. So, I began my walk with God fully at peace with my decision to just have faith in God, and that didn't change when I decided to answer the call and go into ministry. If the Word of God said in Philippians 4:13 that I could do all things through Christ who gave me strength, then my prayer was for Him to give me the strength to do all the things He set on my heart to do. In other words, I chose not to doubt Him. He didn't doubt me when He sent His Son to die for my sins. He changed me, and that was a miracle. He could do anything! So, I chose to just believe what He said.

At the very beginning of my ministry, other preachers I highly respected told me that they didn't think I should do it. A few told me they didn't think I was called to preach, and that even if I was, there would always be "cycles"—times when my ministry would be so dead-broke that I'd need to beg people for money just to keep going. They told me nobody would invite me to preach. In other words, they not only told me what I couldn't do but what God couldn't do either. When I heard those kinds of things, they really rubbed me the wrong way. Of course, I was disappointed that even preachers I highly respected in the faith didn't believe in me, but I was more disappointed that they didn't believe God could take care of the people He called—and I knew I had been called. So, guess what? I chose not to believe them.

From then until now, I've chosen to believe that no matter what is happening in the world around me, God will take care of this ministry that He started. It wasn't always easy, but God always took care of what He placed in my hands. Life has ups and downs, but my faith has not only sustained me, it's protected me and given me a mindset that has paved the way for me to succeed again and again.

The number one problem that I believe plagues believers today is *doubt* about what God can and will do for His children. If you are a new believer, I hope you never learn to do it—and if you've been a Christian for a while and have found yourself caught in doubt's trap, it's time to start actively choosing not to do it.

Doubt is an enemy of growth and a killer of possibilities. Belief is the choice that changes *everything*. Whether it's spiritually, physically, in your relationships with others, or even financially, whatever area it is that you desire to grow, I've found that faith in God always sets you up for success.

Doubt Says You Can't, Faith Says You Can— Doubt Passes the Buck and Shifts the Blame

I came into ministry at a time when just about everybody in the Church was blaming God for something. I refused to do that and it helped me tremendously, but in dealing with others in the Church, I felt like I was swimming against the current.

Many Christians are more comfortable with "can't" than "can"— especially when it relates to God's power to help us through faith. But doubt isn't just the opposite of belief; it's an enemy of belief. A believer who has a habit of doubting God will read a scripture and immediately think, *That won't work*. I've never been that way. Since the day I was born again and started studying the Word, I've always thought, *If God said this, then it will work for me. It may sound crazy. I don't know how He will do it, but I know that if He said He will, then He will.*

I decided very early that if God's Word said He'd supply all my needs according to His riches in glory, like Philippians 4:19 said, then He would. If His Word said in 1 John 4:4 that greater is *He* that is in me than he that is in the world, well, then that is what is true regardless of circumstances. Any scripture I found that told me what I could *be* in Christ, could *have* by obeying His Word, or could *do* if He had put it on my heart was a scripture I decided to believe.

I figured that if it was in the Word, then it wasn't just true in general—but it was true for *me* and was worth *believing*. I remember reading Numbers 3:19 and learning that God was not a man that He should lie. So, I started to see doubting God was like calling Him a liar, and that was something I decided I just wouldn't do. His Word became the final word of wisdom and truth in my mind, and that was just plain that.

I saw a lot of people claiming to be "believers" who always seemed to be in a constant state of blaming God for something or another. You know, so many believers are quick to blame God when they don't see the results they want. It is almost as if they'd rather say something they *know* isn't right (it's God's fault or it's not true) than to say the truth (I don't know what happened yet). I came to realize that the doubt motivating them seemed to have a life of its own! Doubt didn't just affect them from the inside; it seemed to live inside of their mind all the time—and so it not only affected what they thought, but it also affected how they spoke and what they did in life.

Doubt is like a rudder that steers a ship. Doubt is like a disease that ravages hope. Doubt doesn't want the responsibility of believing. Doubt always seems to want to pass the buck or shift the blame—but it's not OK.

Early on, I decided that God knows more than me! If something didn't go the way I planned or wanted, I decided that I wouldn't blame God for what I did or someone else did, or for what I just couldn't understand—and it was not hard for me to think this way. It was just a choice. You see, if you want to live the believer's life in an overcoming way, you are going to have to decide that it's OK not to understand something, but it's *not* OK to blame God.

So, when I heard others either blame God for something or just totally say something against His Word, I'd start thinking to myself, *I just can't do that! God has done too much for me. He saved me from hell on earth and hell after death—He's changed my life and freed me from sin, and He loves me so much . . . and there is nothing in my heart that wants to blame Him for anything!*

Even when I had so little in the early years of ministry and only my wife was on my side, I decided that no matter what the doubters said, God was taking me somewhere good—and that good was all He wanted for me. I believed the Word I found in Jeremiah 29:11 that told me God knew the plans He had for my life, and they were *not* plans for calamity or harm, but *good* plans to give me a future and a hope.

Doubting Is Like Calling God a Liar— I Refuse to Do It, Even If Religious People Do

In the Word, I noticed that there wasn't a single time that Jesus *put* sickness or disease on people; He only healed. I never saw Him encourage debt or praise poverty; He multiplied food, caused nets to overfill, put coins in the fish's mouth, etc. I noticed over and over again how He could work with those who believed—but could do nothing with those who doubted.

When I read the Bible, I get excited and hopeful. It feeds my soul—my mind, will, and emotions. It always has. So, when religious people told me what I *couldn't* do as a believer and a minister, if it was something that God promised but they disagreed with, I considered them for what they were—doubters. Doubting God is like calling Him a liar, and I just refuse to do it even if well-meaning religious people do it all the time. I don't want to be a doubter.

I decided early on that if God said I was the head and not the tail, above and not beneath, then I wasn't going down in life; I was going up. If God said He was for me and not against me, then He was for me even if "they" weren't. If He said He would bless me, then He would, and there was no point for me to get into worry and stress over some future problem "they" predicted was inevitable—because it wasn't.

I decided that I didn't care if everybody had the same cylindrical bad experience in ministry, if God said I could have a different one, then I'd side with God. Those future "cycles" of poverty they warned me about were *not* for me. Consequently, it's just like I said earlier—I never have had that financial deficit they told me "was coming," and I've never had to lay somebody off because I couldn't pay them to work for God!

I never learned to doubt. I had many opportunities, but I didn't want to live that way. I didn't *want* to learn to doubt. I just flat decided that if His Word said He'd bless the work of my hands, then He would do just exactly that. He'd bless me! In the city, in the field, coming in, or going out, I decided that taking Him at His Word was the right thing to do.

Now, sometimes it didn't look like I was getting blessed, but I decided that what I saw would change if I "simply believed" like Jesus Christ taught in the Gospels. I knew that patience would have its perfect work and every promise God made to me would come to pass. I'd reap if I chose to faint not. This is a mindset of faith that I didn't find much in the Church world, but it's what I carried with me everywhere I went.

I've been in fulltime ministry since 1978, and my entire ministry organization is debt free, including all the buildings and all the equipment and tools needed to do our work. My wife, Cathy, has been by my side since the beginning. Our mission is to reach people and change lives, one soul at a time. It's the same mission we've had from the beginning. We love sharing God with others because He's done so much in our lives—we want to see people grow in faith and enjoy good lives here on earth, and make Heaven their eternal home, too.

Our ministry keeps growing every single year, and God keeps giving us new dreams to dream and new visions to accomplish. God has been true to His Word and faithful in every single area we have committed to Him—because that's what never learning to doubt does!

Doubt is dangerous to the plan of God in the life of the believer. I wouldn't be where I am today if I'd developed it, and I'm adamant about never succumbing to it. God is God, and I'm Jesse—and it's not hard to see the difference! I don't argue with that kind of power, and I have just flat decided to put my faith in the One Who made it all and Who gave me the opportunity to do well in life by believing. Anything less than faith is a waste of time and a missed opportunity!

The Most Famous Doubter in the Bible

"DOUBTING THOMAS"

I can't write a book on doubt without talking about the most famous doubter in the Bible—Thomas. Poor Thomas, even his name is now synonymous with doubt! That's what doubting at the wrong moment can do though. It can ruin your reputation, and not just for life but for what may be eternity. I sure hope when we get to Heaven that we let Thomas off the hook. Jesus has forgiven Thomas, so I imagine we all are going to stop calling him "Doubting Thomas" when we get to Heaven!

The contrast between Thomas' *temporary* doubt and Christ's *eternal* victory over sin, hell, death, and the grave is so great. It's so great that most people think Thomas was *always* a doubter. He wasn't. While doubt smeared Thomas's reputation and while his temporary weakness ruined his name, Thomas was a great man in the sight of the Lord.

Remember that Jesus hand-selected Thomas to walk with Him, learn from Him, and be a first-seat-observer of His sacrifice for all of mankind. Jesus liked Thomas. He wanted Thomas as His disciple, and I don't think He wanted him just so that we could make his name mud for all of eternity!

How many people who call themselves believers have doubted Jesus? How many have wanted to *see* something before *believing* something—maybe not publicly, but how many have doubted

Jesus privately? How many have spoken too soon? How many have doubled down on saying something was "impossible" that eventually came to pass? I'd venture to say a great many!

Let's take a look at the scripture now and learn how to be people who don't end up infected, smeared, and known for temporary weaknesses.

When Emotion Clogs Our Ears to the Truth— Mary at the Tomb

Thomas had been following Christ for three solid years when his infamous doubt showed up. The twentieth chapter of the Gospel of John tells the story, and I encourage you to read it for yourself. If you do, you'll learn that at this point in time, Jesus had already been crucified and buried. Mary Magdalene had already been to the grave and saw that the stone covering the grave's entry had been rolled away. She'd run to tell Peter and the rest of the disciples what she saw, and they had run back with her to find an empty grave—there was no body in the tomb, and just the linen that had been wrapped around Jesus after His crucifixion was all that lay in the grave.

Mary had gone back to the tomb again. She was crying by the tomb when two angels showed up to ask why she was crying. When she said what she assumed had happened (that someone had come and taken Jesus' body away and laid Him somewhere else), that is when the Lord appeared to her—which completely shocked her. Wouldn't *you* be shocked? Here you go to see a loved one who's passed and the stone is rolled away, angels are standing there, and there's no body to be found. What would you think? Mary thought what anybody would think, that someone had stolen the body or moved the body. She was totally fixed on the body. Why? Because she couldn't imagine a resurrection. That was an impossibility in her mind, just like it'd be an impossibility in anybody's mind.

Mary had seen Jesus crucified with her own eyes. She knew without a shadow of a doubt that her Lord was dead—and so when Christ appeared and started talking to her, asking her the same question as the angel, Mary didn't fathom that she was actually hearing the voice of Jesus. Why? Because it was an impossibility to her. Because she was emotionally distraught and grieving a new problem—not only that her savior had been killed and taken from her, but that someone may have come and taken even His very body from her.

I want you to see that when our emotions are spinning and our mind is solely focused on the problems, it's hard to hear the voice of God. Mary was so troubled that even though Jesus was talking to her, she didn't recognize Him. She wasn't even looking at Him. She was looking at the problem—the tomb, the missing body. She was looking at what she lacked, when everything she wanted was right there in front of her.

Her mind was so fixed on His missing earthly body that she mistook the voice of Jesus for what she assumed was a caretaker at the gravesite. It wasn't until Jesus called her name with force, "Mary!" that He got her attention off the problem—only then did she turn and recognize Who she was talking to. Jesus, the answer to the problem, was right in front of her eyes.

"Rabbi!" she cried, and immediately tried to run and cling to Him. Jesus stopped Mary in her tracks and told her not to touch Him. You see, Jesus had not yet ascended to His Father in Heaven. Now, why He didn't want to be touched until He ascended is a mystery we may not fully understand until we get to Heaven, but Jesus was adamant about it and Mary heeded His request. From this we know that Jesus wasn't just revealing Himself in Spirit. He had a body, a physical and touchable body, whose purity and integrity He wanted to preserve until His ascension to His Father in Heaven.

You Can't See, Hear, or Be Filled
If You Don't "Show Up"—Thomas

The resurrection is the birth of Christianity. Without the resurrection and without people *knowing* about the resurrection by actually seeing Jesus after His death, there would be no Christianity as we know it today. Jesus would have gone down in history as another moral teacher persecuted by opposing men. But Jesus was not just a moral teacher, and His revealing Himself after death to so many was a purposeful and needful thing. When Jesus showed up after death, it changed everything.

Jesus left Mary at the tomb, and when He did, she quickly went to tell the disciples what had just happened. Jesus appeared again that very evening to the disciples. Now, you have to remember that the disciples were living in fear of those who'd killed Jesus—His death had just happened, and while they were worried that just assembling together would bring them persecution, they still showed up.

In secret, they closed the door to the place were they'd gathered to talk, and then Jesus again appears—just like He appeared to Mary, He appeared to the disciples . . . but one person was missing from the group. Can you guess who it was? It was Thomas. Thomas was not with them that night, and so he didn't see Jesus appear. Thomas was still under the impression that Christ was dead and lying in the tomb while his brothers in the faith spoke to the risen Christ.

So when Jesus spoke to the disciples, Thomas didn't hear it. When Jesus showed the disciples His hands and feet—the marks of His crucifixion visible on His body—Thomas didn't see it. Again, you can read the story in John 20 for yourself, but I want you to notice that Thomas didn't see what Mary or the other disciples saw or hear what they heard, and when Jesus breathed on them and said, "Receive the Holy Spirit," all of them received His Spirit . . . except Thomas. Why? Because Thomas wasn't there. And lastly, when Jesus commissioned them all to go out with the message of forgiveness of sins, Thomas wasn't there to hear that message.

So, Thomas didn't see anything or hear anything, and he wasn't filled with anything. No sight. No power. No commission, which meant no purpose. What's one lesson we can learn from this for our own lives today, beyond the actual story? The message is that you can't get anything unless you show up! Showing up is half the battle, and Thomas just didn't show up.

If Thomas had visited the tomb, he would have seen what Mary saw. If he'd risked persecution and gathered with the other disciples, he would have received what they received. He would have been given the direction he needed—and not later on, but right then with his other brothers and sisters in the faith. Thomas would have found his purpose for the next phase of his life, and guess what? We never would have heard a word about him having doubts about Jesus. All he had to do was show up!

When Thomas Started to Show Up,
a Resurrected Christ Showed Up

Thomas loved Jesus. He was with Him for three years, and the disciples were all close to one another—so when Thomas wasn't a part of the group, they didn't just leave him alone. They reached out to tell him what had happened. The disciples wanted Thomas to know that Jesus had risen from the dead, that He was alive and well. They weren't about to leave their friend out of the loop.

This is the passage that made Thomas famous and why he became known as "Doubting Thomas." John 20:24-25 says, *"But Thomas, one of the twelve, called Didymus, was not with them when Jesus came. The other disciples therefore said unto him, We have seen the Lord. But he said unto them, Except I shall see in His hands the print of the nails, and put my finger into the print of the nails, and thrust my hand into His side, I will not believe."*

What is the difference between doubt and faith? It's when we hear the truth and still refuse to believe it. Thomas loved Jesus, remember that. He wasn't a bad man; he was a great man . . . with a momentary lapse of faith. The difference is that he spoke his doubt. He didn't just question if it was true; he made a declaration that he not only didn't believe Jesus' words, but he also didn't believe the disciples' words.

Even though Thomas had seen the miracles Jesus had done in His ministry, even though he'd heard Jesus say that He would rise again, and even though he was hearing that his friends, the disciples and Mary, had seen Jesus alive . . . he refused to believe any of it. But do you want to know what is funny about this story? Thomas started showing up anyway!

Oh, Thomas was there, buddy! I bet he never left the group, ha! And do you know what happened? When Thomas started showing up, Jesus started showing up again. John 20:26: *"And after eight days again His disciples were within, and Thomas with them: then came Jesus, the doors being shut, and stood in the midst, and said, Peace be unto you."* It took *eight* days.

Notice that when Mary said to the disciples that she'd seen Jesus, they believed and assembled—and Jesus showed up that night. When Thomas heard it and doubted it so hard that he said, "Uh-uh! You let me see the hands and feet and then I'll believe!" (paraphrase), Jesus didn't show up again for *eight* days. Sometimes you have to wait longer when you choose doubt. Faith is the currency of God, and if you let doubt rule and keep saying it, you can't even get what God wants for you.

Thomas was showing up though at this point, and I love what Jesus says when He appears to them all on that eighth day—*"Peace be unto you!"* Who do you think He was saying that to? Everybody! Everybody heard that blessing of peace, that command to be at peace, but who do you think it affected most? Doubt will suck the peace right out of you, and I believe Jesus' choice of words was a proclamation mainly meant for the one with the least peace about seeing Him—the only one in the room that was seeing Him as the risen Christ for the first time. Thomas! In fact, it's Thomas who Jesus immediately addresses first before He says anything else to the group.

Jesus Took Thomas' Doubt and Made It a Message of Faith

John 20:27-28: *"Then saith He to Thomas, Reach hither thy finger, and behold My hands; and reach hither thy hand, and thrust it into My side: and be not faithless, but believing. And Thomas answered and said to Him, My Lord and my God!"*

What was Thomas doing at this point? He was unlearning doubt! Jesus was proving Himself, using the same words Thomas had used to doubt Him—that is love and mercy in action. It was a sovereign act of grace being extended to the most doubtful in the group. But notice that Jesus was teaching him right in the same moment with the statement: *"be not faithless, but believing."* That was a teaching moment. It was Jesus answering Thomas not only by just *showing* Him the wounds, but by giving him the *words* he would need for the rest of his life if he never wanted to be a doubter of God's power again.

You see, the others didn't doubt in the same way that Thomas did—they didn't have that down-in-their-soul kind of doubt. There is a difference between thoughts that you temporarily have and thoughts that you choose to speak and keep. Jesus took Thomas' doubt and turned it into a message on faith! Like the Good Shepherd Who left the ninety-nine for the one, Jesus turned His attention to the one in the room who needed to regain His faith in God's ability to do anything—including Jesus' ability as God's Son to fulfill every single jot and tittle of His Word.

Jesus had called this man for a purpose, and we can see why by his response to not only the sight of Christ but the message of Christ, *"be not faithless, but believing"*—because Thomas doesn't make an excuse for his doubt. He says nothing about his own weakness or humanity. He doesn't give an excuse why he wasn't at the grave or with the other disciples the time before. All he does is immediately correct the problem by reaffirming his faith with these simple words: *"My* LORD *and my God!"*

"My" Lord and "my" God is *personal*. Three years before that day, when Thomas had chosen to walk away from his way of life to follow Jesus, that too was personal. This man had a personal relationship with Jesus. So, just as his doubt was so deep and personal, his declaration was also deep and personal—he made an immediate reaffirmation of his faith in Jesus Christ as *his* Lord and God as *his* Father.

If you doubt deeply, if you speak it and dig in your heels, then be the kind of believer who receives correction the way Thomas did—don't make an excuse. If you blew it and you know it, just turn it around and make it personal. It's not important "why" you didn't believe—God already knows your every "why" before you try to make it sound good. Just hear the words of Jesus to you, *"be not faithless, but believing"* and make that simple return to *"My* LORD *and my God!"*

The present tense "ing" in *believing* tells us that our faith should be ongoing and always at work in our lives. If you go back and forth between unbelieving and believing all the time, you'll lose your peace of mind. A double-minded person is unstable in all his ways—so refuse to dig in your heels with doubt. The less you do that, the less you'll need correcting, and the more peace of mind you will have every day.

The Story of Thomas Was Recorded for *One* Reason

What Jesus says next is the last thing He says to Thomas that is recorded in the Word, and it's a jewel that we should all take to heart if we want to live a blessed life. John 20:29: *"Jesus saith unto him, Thomas, because thou hast seen Me, thou hast believed: blessed are they that have not seen, and yet have believed."*

The Word goes on to say, *"And many other signs truly did Jesus in the presence of His disciples, which are not written in this book: But these are written, that ye might believe that Jesus is the Christ, the Son of God; and that believing ye might have life through His name"* (John 20:30-31).

You see, although Jesus did many other signs that day, this story of Thomas and the words of Jesus were recorded for one reason: that we may *believe* that Jesus Christ is the Son of God, and that in that *believing* we may have *life* in His name.

Eternal life is one part of that *life* Jesus came to give, but it isn't the only kind of life we need—we need life right here and now as we go through this earthly experience, too. John 10:10 makes it clear that there is an enemy of God at work in the world. Jesus compares this enemy to a thief whose aim is to do three things, which are to steal, kill, and destroy us. But Jesus said that He is the opposite of all of that. Jesus said that He came to be a Giver. He came that we might have life, and life more abundantly.

Doubt's first theft was mankind's position—that was in the Garden. Doubting God is a form of satanic pollution. I believe that it is Satan's greatest weapon because it gets our eyes off of God and onto just our natural senses. Doubt always comes out of the five senses. Thomas' demand to see Jesus' hands, to put his finger in the holes, and thrust his hand in His side in order to believe is an example of how doubt always relies on the senses. Jesus wants us to rely on our faith—and more blessing follows those who don't see and yet still believe.

The blessed and abundant life Jesus came to give is a *believing* life; not a doubting life. It's a life that trusts God over the natural senses. If we make a soul-deep doubting mistake like Thomas, we can course-correct ourselves and turn back to the *believing* life just like Thomas did, too. Better than even that, we can choose to be someone who never has to course-correct ourselves back to faith . . . because we never doubted Jesus in the first place.

Doubt Isn't a Fleeting Thought or a Questioning Mind

IT'S A DELIBERATE AND REPETITIVE CHOICE TO NOT BELIEVE GOD

Doubt is not just a questioning mind. Doubt isn't just a fleeting thought. The type of doubt I'm talking about is the doubt about God that you repeat to yourself over and over until it drops into your heart.

True doubt is when you allow thoughts that contradict what God has said in His Word to remain active—and it's that kind of repetitiveness, whether it is a repetitive denial of what God said or of who He created you to be, that can wreak havoc on your joy and peace of mind.

If you want to have peace or joy, if you want to see God's Word work for you, and if you want to accomplish something He's put on your heart, then what you repetitively say to yourself is important.

If you question in order to learn more, you're not doubting—you're trying to *learn* and *receive* more. But if you question in order to *dismiss* God's Word, then you are on the opposing side of truth and just using questions as a ruse. There's a difference. It's all about intention.

The Philippians 4:8 Thought List

The more you think something, the greater it becomes in your own mind, which is why the Word tells us to think on things that fall into certain categories. Philippians 4:8 lists them: *". . . whatsoever things are true, whatsoever things are honest, whatsoever things are just, whatsoever things are pure, whatsoever things are lovely, whatsoever things are of good report; if there be any virtue, and if there be any praise, think on these things."*

Peace of mind comes when you repetitively choose thoughts that bring you peace of mind. Philippians 4:8 is a thought list, and if you want peace of mind, the thoughts you repeat in your head should fall into one or more of the categories in that list. Remember, God wouldn't tell you to *"think on these things"* if you didn't have the ability to do it—so don't accept "I can't" if that wrong idea comes into your head. He wouldn't have said you should unless you could! Besides, it's in your best interest. It's not good to walk around wracked with thoughts that rob your peace.

I've made up my mind that thoughts may come in to rob me of peace, but I will not let them stay. Whatever doesn't fit into those categories may come, but they have to go just as quickly! Doubting God just doesn't fit into God's advice to "think on these things"—and besides, repetitively rehearsing a problem never gets rid of a problem. Whatever you think about all the time becomes what you believe, talk about, and act on—so why would you want to place your focus on what you don't want? Rehearse the answer, not the problem.

Never learning to doubt is about choosing God's Word and what's best over whatever thoughts come up that go against His Word. Whether it's something you hear or your own inner dialogue, ask yourself if it fits into Philippians 4:8. Is it true, honest, just, or pure? Is it lovely or of a good report? Is there any virtue or could any praise come from that thought? If not, decide that it's not "your thought"— that's what I do and it works. It forces me to confront things from a perspective of light and not from a perspective of darkness.

I Believe in Pushing the Light and Letting the Light Do Its Work

In general, I don't fight darkness in the world; I push the light. I don't fight what Jesus already won. The devil is a defeated foe. I enforce his defeat by continually pushing what is light and good, knowing that darkness flees in the face of light. So, I walk in Christ's victory by pushing the light of *His* words and *His* ways.

I don't conquer darkness by thinking or talking about all the darkness. Dark doesn't go away by talking about it. Awareness isn't enough. We have to do something, and that something is pushing the light. Again, light will push out darkness, but many believers are more interested in *talking* about the darkness, *worrying* about the darkness, *warning* everybody about the darkness! Some are even interested in making money off of the darkness! That's not good. It's just filling our minds with what we don't want in the first place—it's just perpetuating the problem by rehearsing the problem. I believe in pushing the light and letting the light do its work.

Let Jesus' truths work in you, and watch how darkness recoils. There is no peace in dark thoughts. However, there is plenty of peace in the light of God's Word—but it is up to us to push that light! And this is as much about choosing to dwell on light-filled *thoughts* as it is on good words and deeds.

Nobody Can Take Away What You Don't Give Them Access To

Your mind is the preparation zone for the life you will lead and the emotions you'll feel. It's the prep-zone for the day you are going to have—sometimes it's even the preparation for the moment you're going to experience next. *You* determine how you are going to feel by the thoughts that you think in repetition.

All emotions are generated by the thoughts in your head. If you get mad at some woman in church, you may think it's what sister so-and-so did that ruined your mood and hijacked your day. You may go to bed with her on your mind and think she stole your whole day. In actuality, you gave up your own day by allowing her words to stick around in your head all day. By repeating the thoughts of whatever she said or did over and over, you chose to keep on creating that original emotion throughout the day. That's what ruined your mood all day long, because sister so-and-so wasn't there all day. She left, but you kept her close in your own mind. Do you understand what I'm saying with this example?

Nobody can take away what you don't give them access to. So, when thoughts arise that don't fit that Philippians 4:8 list, put the wall up! Say, "No, that's not for me . . . I'm having a good day because I'm choosing to have a free mind." You don't have to be in prison to your own emotions—you take back your thoughts and you'll take back your emotions. Even if the problems are outside of you, what you rehearse inside of you is what determines your emotions.

So, don't ignore the reality that repetitive doubtful thoughts can lead you astray or rob you of joy. Doubt is like a cancer cell. It isn't going to help you or keep you from pain—doubt will just turn on you like cancer eating away at your best self. Don't let doubtful thoughts multiply and steal your peace. Don't give doubt access to your mind—kick it out.

Do you ever notice how doubt sometimes tries to gain entry in the late hours when you are supposed to be lying down for rest? Do you notice how sometimes doubt tries to hit you first thing in the morning when you are supposed to be waking up to a brand-new day? Notice how fear will try to bookend your days. It's no coincidence.

The brain loves to problem solve; it'll even come up with imaginary problems just so it can try to figure out the worst-case scenarios. Have you ever noticed that? If you let thoughts run wild, it can ruin your sleep before bed or cause you to dread the day before you even get out of bed. Not me! I've come to see all that as just fear and doubt—and I refuse to let rogue thoughts separate me from my faith. I will not make a habit of doubting God's Word.

The Word says in Psalm 4:8 that we can lie down in peaceful rest. In Proverbs 12:25 it says that anxiety in the heart of a man weighs him down—but what makes him glad? A good word. Isaiah 26:3 gives us the key when it says, *Thou wilt keep him in perfect peace, whose mind is stayed on Thee: because he trusteth in Thee.* What you allow to stay in your mind matters. You see, doubt works from the inside out. Faith works from the outside in.

What you put in can build you up or tear you down. You get weaker when you focus on the thoughts inside your mind that doubt God. You get stronger inside when you choose to hear God's Word over and over. Joshua 1:8 even describes how success and prosperity are linked to meditating on God's Word. In other words, faith for anything God promises in His Word is something built practically by taking an "outside" thing (the Word) and putting it inside your own ears and mind on a consistent basis. So, it's something easy that you can do every single day.

Remember that the Word is living and active. The only way to build faith in God is to *hear* God's Word—which is about more than just reading a scripture. It's about the habit of reminding yourself of what you've read. It's not words on a page; it's words of life for those who receive it. It's God's way of showing you how life really works. It's His advice to you on how to live and have peace and joy in this life, even as you encounter challenges.

The world is filled with wishy-washy people and there are so many voices and ideas vying for you attention—but it's just that unfocused way of living that makes most people miserable.

I Bookend My Days with Good Words

One way I prep my mind is by bookending my days with what's good. I believe that the first thing you hear in the morning and the last thing you hear before bed are more important than most people realize. I believe we do our best when we choose good things right before bed and good things right when we wake up. So, I deliberately put scriptures in my mind every single day. I rely on them for not only the spiritual strength but for the mental strength they give me.

Who knows what the day will bring? I expect good, but if something negative comes up, I expect that God will work it out for good in my life—that I will triumph in Christ over whatever tries to shake me. I don't doubt 2 Corinthians 2:14. That verse tells me God will always lead me to triumph in Christ.

Now, I can't be led to triumph if I'm not following God's lead, and I won't know where He's going if I don't listen—so I listen. If He says His Word is a light unto my path, then it's important for me to put the Word in every single day. It's the light I need for living this life, and I know it. I make His Word the first thing I read and hear in the morning. I make it the last thing I read and hear before bed too, because I want even my sleep to begin with something good!

The Word has a way of focusing your thoughts onto what is good and what matters. When you make it a morning and night habit, you are starting your day and ending it with words of life—not words of death, destruction, doubt, and the scattered ideas of the world.

What you focus on changes your perspective. It's hard to have faith if all you fill up on are the doubtful words and ideas of the world—you have to combat that onslaught either by turning the doubt off entirely or just doing what I do, making sure the Word is first place above all the other noise.

I like to know what's going on in the world. I watch the news. I read. I keep up. But it doesn't destroy my peace because I make God's Word my centerpoint and focus. What they say can't kill my mood because I'm in charge of my mood, not the news!

I don't let misery remain in my head, even if I see it. No, I pray for what I see, I pray for people and situations, our leaders, the countries of the world, etc., but I work to always focus my mind back to God's Word. That's where my answer lies, and that's where my peace lies. There's no point in me taking on the burden of worry when the Prince of Peace lives inside of me. His light pushes out darkness, even in my own mind. Why should I keep rehearsing the problem when God has given me the answer in the Holy Spirit that's residing within me through the miracle work of salvation? I find and keep my strength in the Lord, not in the world!

It's Hard to Doubt When You Take Ownership of the Word

People seem to come to me when everything is falling apart in their lives. When the world seems to be going down, I find ministers calling me left and right—they want to know what I think or what God is telling me in troubled times. They come to me for encouragement and to be lifted up, and they often seem amazed that I'm not discouraged or worrying when everything seems to be hitting the fan. They think I have great faith. Guess what? I do! I've become a voice in troubled times, and I think it is because I never learned to doubt.

Doubt is a time-stealer just as much as it's a peace-killer. I don't have just plain old confidence. I have faith, and that's something anybody can have. Let me tell you, it's only God's Word that has given me the resolute mindset that I have today—I'm not interested in what the world thinks as much as I'm interested in what God has already said. My focus isn't scattered, and that's why my mind doesn't freak out when troubles come or the world starts seeming to go nuts.

I don't give up because I don't believe in giving up. God didn't give up on me; I'm not giving up on God. God doesn't doubt that I am here; I don't doubt that He is here! From the minute I got saved to now, God has been with me—and He will be with me into eternity. So, even when everything looks bad, my focus is on how God is going to show up and show out! "They" can say whatever they want about how bad it's going to get. Guess what? I want to look at how *good* it's going to get—because God said He's going to lead me to triumph in Christ. Not every believer is going to triumph—only those being led in Christ, which is something the triumphant believer aims to do every day. Part of the triumphant believer's lifestyle includes *not* doubting God's Word all the time. You see, I don't doubt the One Who is leading me to triumph—and that's probably why people call me so much when troubled times in the world occur. I always become very popular in a time of crisis! Why? Because times of crisis require strength, and there is no greater strength than faith in the light at the end of the tunnel!

You see, when you never learn to doubt, you don't waste as much time spinning in circles in your own head about how bad everything is—you use that time to remind yourself and others about what God said, no matter what the devil is doing. I use my time for dreaming new dreams, giving new gifts, doing new things, and just plain loving people, or enjoying my life and work. I don't waste it on spinning in doubt. Again, doubt doesn't have answers. It just has more questions.

The More You Build Yourself Up in the Word, the Less Effort It Takes to Do It

So, I quote scripture to myself in the morning. I use the Word to build me up through the day as I need it. At one time, when I was beginning to build this habit, it was a conscious effort to speak good things over myself. Now, it's just something I do without thinking. It's just like any other habit. The more you do it, the less effort it takes to do it. It's become like autopilot for me. I suggest it becomes the same for you.

You see, it's easy to stand strong when the world is going to hell in a handbasket if your habit is to instantly turn to God—to immediately flip your mind from what "they" say to what God says. When that becomes second nature to you, and it's not just something you say but something you believe, it's amazing how much easier it gets handling the winds of change in this world. It's also amazing how popular you get with people who need encouragement. You become like a magnet for those in need of good words. They may not understand your joy, but they seek you to experience a little of it.

It's very hard to doubt God and your own good future when you are filling your mind with, "No weapon formed against me will prosper—nothing people do to harm me will succeed in the end. God, You are always with me! I've found Your wisdom and it's always bringing me life and favor. I'm blessed everywhere I go! I'm more than a conqueror! If You are for me, God, who can be against me?"

It's hard to keep up a habit of doubt when you are saying things to yourself like, "I eat the fat of the land and I drink what is good. I share with those who have nothing and recognize the holiness of each day. I choose not to be sad because the joy of the Lord is my strength! I walk by faith and not by sight. I'm not moved by what I see; I'm moved by what I believe, and I believe God!"

So when the world rocks, I don't fall apart. I'm not stronger inside than anybody else, but I have trained my mind. You see, when I read a verse like, 'if a thousand fall at my side or 10,000 at my right, no harm will come to me because God is with me,' I take it to heart (Psalm 91:7). I choose to believe that God is with me when the world is shaking. Even if a dire situation arises, I believe that God will give me the grace I need, the peace I need, and the protection I need—He will show me His salvation. One way or another, He will make sure I am all right! Thinking this way doesn't just happen. It's created by habit first, and then by keeping up the habit as a lifestyle.

Notice that I put *myself* inside the scripture. I take ownership over it. You see, I know that favor from God will bring me what money can't buy, so I speak favor over my life because the scripture says I'm favored. His mercy, kindness, and truth are written on my heart and bound around my neck like Proverbs 3:3 says, and they help me find favor, good understanding, and high esteem in the sight of *both* God and man. So, I say I have favor coming from all sides! I speak that over my life and that's how God's Word becomes written on my heart or bound around my neck, so to speak.

I Never Learned to Doubt God Will Bless Me

I also know that it's God Who gives me the power to create wealth, so I just plain believe that, too (Deuteronomy 8:18). I know when God gives blessings because they come with no sorrow attached— so that's what I decided would happen to me. I don't accept that sorrow must go hand in hand with money, because God said that when it comes from Him, it just doesn't (Proverbs 10:22).

I know that a lot of believers are afraid of money, but I'm not one of them. They think it's evil, but they still work for it and still want more of it—I don't think money is evil at all. First Timothy 6:10 says that it is the *love* of money that is the root of evil. Love is the subject of that verse. It's talking about the evils of giving your *love* to money. Money itself is just a tool and a blessing, and you can help more people with it than without it. *Loving* money is evil because it puts a person into a mindset that they should be *devoted* to money—and you should never *love* something intangible that can't possibly love you back.

Love is a strong word that means something. It's not the throw-away word people have diluted it to today. God *is* love. If you *love* money, you are making it a *replacement* for God. You can't substitute God for money and be happy, no matter how many possessions you have. The good thing is, you can have both—look through the scriptures and you'll find the "blessing of God" was very often equated to wealth, and followed those who were righteous and *believed.*

My God, my wife, my family, and other people—that's who I reserve my love for, so I have no problem praying for finances, believing for finances, or quoting scriptures about finances to build my faith. I already know my love is not reserved for paper money or even the things money buys. I keep my love separate from my money! I don't fear it either. Why? Because I know that God will freely give me all the things I want just for pure *enjoyment* so long as I put Him first, don't doubt His words, and let my faith lead me in His good ways of living (Romans 8:32; 1 Timothy 6:17).

It's Not a Hard Choice to Choose What's Good for My Soul

All this isn't a pep talk. God's Word is living, active, and sharper than any two-edged sword—so all I'm doing is sowing the words of life (Hebrews 4:12). Life has energy. God's Word is full of the energy of life. That's why it activates my faith more than anybody else's words. I could just repeat a great quote from somebody I like, but even if the quote were great and wise, it wouldn't have the life-energy and power of God's Word.

If I was at a restaurant and they only had two things on the menu, and one of them was obviously better, I'd choose what was better. Wouldn't you? Let's say they brought me two bowls—one filled with my favorite gumbo and the other one filled with nothing, just empty—do you think I'd take the *empty* bowl? No, I love gumbo! My point is that having the self-discipline to study the Word and then put myself into the scriptures—to stir up the gift inside of me and lift me up—isn't a hard choice for me because I know that I'm choosing what's good for my soul. So, when I pick up the Word, I know I'm picking up refreshment for my soul. Nothing compares to that for advancing in life and crushing any doubt that tries to infringe upon my faith.

Whatever you do on a consistent basis is going to change you. So, when you mix the mental discipline of refusing to doubt with a consistent intake of the Word, it's like a double whammy for your day, which, little by little, changes your life.

If you aren't in the habit, then get into the habit! What may seem like a small amount of time to devote to your soul's well-being in the moment compounds. Before you know it, your craving for your own well-being overturns your former craving for the distractions that once kept you from it. Why? It's because when you start paying attention to your spirit and really read the Word with the intention of receiving, your spirit connects with God's Spirit in a greater way. It's not like just good words or even just gaining wisdom; it's developing your relationship—spirit to Spirit—with God and His life-giving nature.

If people have starved themselves spiritually, they are living a one-sided life—dictated by their flesh only. They may not even realize the nourishment they are missing and they've just got a habit of only craving fleshly distractions. Again, whatever you do consistently becomes your craving to do consistently. That's all a habit is.

If you find that your spiritual energy is low, you can get out of the rut just by realizing you need to feed your spirit. The more I meditate on God's Word, not only does it nourish my spirit and strengthen my faith, but it also gives me more energy in life.

Believing Has Made My Spirit Strong and My Heart Young

I am not interested in retiring—ever. I keep a traveling schedule that most people twenty to thirty years younger say they couldn't keep. I still get on the treadmill, I still enjoy my life, and I don't feel much different than when I was 40 years old. So many young people I've met tell me, "You're not old . . . I mean, something about you just isn't old." I laugh because I know they see my face, they may have grown up hearing me preach, and they know I'm old in years. They want to know why I'm the way I am.

I think a lifestyle of never learning to doubt has kept my heart young. It's probably helped to keep me energetic in my mind more than anything external that I do. My spirit is strong. I'm still interested in life because the God inside of me is interested in life! You see, it's not religion that keeps me going strong; it's my faith and openness to the feeding of my spirit.

Believing God's Word has a life-producing effect—not just reading or talking about it, but believing it. I think believing affects the whole of a person—spirit, soul, and body. I believe the Word when it says the Lord will renew my strength like the eagle's (Isaiah 40:29-

31; Psalm 103:5). Check out my hair. Have you seen a bald eagle? We have this white-headed look in common!

Soaring like the eagles can't happen if your mind is stuck on pecking with the chickens, as they say. You have to get up to the high places in your mind, and for me, keeping my relationship with the Lord first-place is what takes me to those high places.

Fill your mind repetitively with what's good and don't let the low-lying distractions stick around in your head—give yourself the opportunity to think higher and grow in wisdom. Not only will you see everything that happens in life from a better perspective, but you'll also end up with more opportunities than you might think to influence others for the better, too.

Doubt Is an Ambition-Killer

IT HIDES IN OVERTHINKING, PROCRASTINATING, AND FALSE SELF-PROTECTION

Some people secretly believe that if they doubt God's Word—if they lower their expectations—it will somehow protect them from future disappointment. They are scared to put their faith in God "in case it doesn't work." So, they choose doubt and don't do anything in faith.

Nobody can avoid pain or disappointment in life, and fear of failure is still just fear—and fear is something you can overcome and something which you should shun. If you never do something with the faith God gave you (and He's given all of us a measure of faith), you'll never know what God can do for you. You'll never prove to yourself what's possible with God. You won't get to experience what He really has in store for you. Personally, I don't want to live fearing anything that God says is possible for His children, so I don't.

Faith Gives You the Courage to Take Off the Limits

I've come to see doubt in all sorts of things that hinder the believer's progress—and, I have to tell you, it's hiding everywhere. Doubt is an ambition-killer. It hides in overthinking. It camouflages itself as concern or practicality. Doubt masquerades as self-protection, too—but, really, it's just fear.

Faith is childlike. Doubt is the opposite. Doubt muddies the believer's mind and is a killer of focus. The overthinking version of doubt is like a pinball machine that robs you of energy to move forward in your life. It keeps you turning in circles, making sure you don't go anywhere of value in your own mind. If you let it continually spin you in circles, it'll also rob you of the passion you *need* to exercise great expectation in God's Word, and great faith in His plan for your life. It'll steal your future blessings, too, if you let it. Don't let it.

I don't want my faith hindered by fear. I don't want my ambition wiped out by overthinking. And I don't want to sit around doing nothing when God has given me so much to do! This is the life I've been given, and I want to live it well. I can think of no better way than to live in faith and enter Heaven knowing I aimed for God's best in my life—that I did what was set before me. When I cross over to Heaven one day, I want to hear, "Well done, good and faithful servant" and not, "Well . . . what have you done?"

Doubt doesn't get much done. Doubt plays it safe and "tries." Trying doesn't get much done! Think about it. If you ask somebody to come to an event you're planning and they say, "I'll try," do you think they are coming? Everybody knows that chances are they aren't coming. The "I'll try" mindset is another one of those things that is just a cover for doubt.

Human nature likes a way out, and doubt gives people that way out. But if you want to do what God has put on your heart, or if you want to have what God has said you can have in His Word—whether it's spiritual, physical, financial, or in your relationships—you will *have* to have guts. You'll have to choose courage over comfort and push aside the natural mind's desire to overthink God's Word, lower expectations, and hide out in procrastination.

Don't lower your expectations thinking you are protecting yourself. That's a lie; it's a false and imaginary thing. Just see it for what it is: *Fear.* God is with you, He's behind you, and you have what it takes to believe for His best in your life. You really *can* do all things through Christ who gives you strength—and He will give you strength. He'll never leave you or forsake you. You'll never be alone in your faith.

The Holy Spirit will always be with you, nudging you to take the limits off. Be willing to be brave—because bravery is worth it. Anybody can live a boring, faithless, low-expectation life—but God has called you to be braver than that. Always remember that as a believer, you will *do* more and *have* more from God if you first *believe* more. If you believe less, then you'll do and have less, too.

A Child Has to Be *Taught* to Doubt— We All Start Out with Childlike Faith

A child has to be taught to doubt—because when they are young, they simply believe they "can," and they get highly upset if you tell them they "can't." A child never wants to hear "no." They want to climb to the top of the slide and go down as fast as they can because they do not fear the ride down. They know that if they fall it might hurt, but they'll get back up—and give the slide another shot, and another shot, and another! They don't quit as easily as some adults do. Why? Because they haven't yet learned to doubt so much.

When we come to God, we are usually older and have had a lifetime of being told what we *can't* do. Sometimes Christians are the worst when it comes to downplaying or flat-out denying God's ability or will to perform His Word—many are just stuck in the habit of trying to protect themselves from some future disappointment.

Others just keep replaying their own past in their mind, just telling themselves it's evidence of what they can't have or can't do in the future. They not only have learned to doubt, but they've become such masters at it that they think it's their responsibility to spread the doubt-disease around!

Old patterns can be broken—and doubt is a pattern that needs to be broken to succeed with God. Faith is the currency of God and it's what He requires if you want to live and do things His way. It's built through hearing the Word of God, and that means that anybody can do it. Deciding to never learn to doubt is joyful because living by childlike faith is a much more hopeful and open way to live. We aren't God's adults, you know. We are God's *children*. Putting our faith in Him is how we were created to live.

Have you ever noticed that children usually don't walk around confused and miserable all the time, unless someone is not treating or training them right? Well, doubt is a bad trainer, and it sure doesn't treat you right! Doubting leads to confusion, and that can end up being debilitating. Believing, on the other hand, has an energy to it that is so much more hopeful—it's freeing and childlike. Believing laughs in the face of what doubt fears, and it is a much easier way to live in my opinion.

We Are Limited without God and Stifled without Faith

I like hearing the word "can." "Can't" is just doubt's way of trying to take me for a ride and rob me of my position as God's child—because childlike faith is supposed to be my default position!

I figure, what's the point of telling yourself you "can't" if God said that with Him, you "can"? Too many believers walk around constantly reinforcing the lie that they "can't." If you do this, I have a question for you. Do you think if you *say* "I can't" long enough that you'll somehow convince God you are right? God will always believe that with Him, you can—He's not changing!

What God says about you in His Word is the truth. If *you* say something different about yourself, then the bottom line is that you aren't telling the truth—you are just lying to yourself. God says you can do *all* things through Christ Who gives you strength, and childlike faith believes that and then goes out and ends up proving it true.

You see, we are limited without God and stifled without faith. Once we find God and start living the believing life, we have access to God and access to strength we never had before. It's an inner strength that only He can give—peace that is hard to understand, joy even in trouble, and guidance that no man or woman on this earth, no matter how talented or wise, can provide. We can start living by faith and not just by sight, in His strength and not just our own, and we can use His divine principles in His Word to do things a different way—a believing way.

Childlike faith is so much the opposite of doubt. Doubt feels like we are hammering at our dreams or goals alone, but childlike faith knows we are never alone or forsaken. God is with us. We don't have to come up with all the strategies. We have a whole Bible full of life-strategies and a power source called the Holy Spirit inside us to comfort and guide us. We can move forward each day with hope instead of fear . . . unless, of course, you choose doubt.

Doubt Is a Blindfold—
It Keeps You from Seeing What's Possible

A lot of people call themselves a believer, but they don't believe much of anything that Jesus said. If you listen to them long enough, you'll be able to tell. A "play it safe" or "zero expectation" mindset isn't hard to spot. It's marked by a habit of fixating on problems instead of what God said, and a tendency to dismiss or water down whatever concept of faith Jesus taught. In other words, it holds on to a form of godliness but denies the power of godliness. It's a bunch of nice sounding words, but underneath those words is doubt in God's power.

You get what you consistently believe for, and you see what you consistently want to see. It's always our choice how we view things. I like to see through the eyes of faith in God because I know that doubt is a blindfold—it doesn't want you to see what is possible with God.

People have always tried to get me to lower my expectations. I can't tell you how many times I've heard, "Now, don't get crazy with this thing . . ." But I just believe that if "getting crazy with this thing" means having faith in the principles of God, call me crazy! If it means believing what Jesus said, then, again, call me crazy. I don't want to be blindfolded by doubt. I know with God that all things are possible.

Many of the people I ministered alongside in my early years, who tried to get me to lower my expectations or called me crazy, are long out of the ministry. Now they come and look at what God has done in my ministry and don't call me crazy anymore. They sit on my "crazy" every time they put their butts on my "debt-free/owe-no-man-any-thing-but-to-love-him" pew! Hallelujah! They got the results of their faith, and I got the results of mine. I'm not better than them, and they aren't better than me, but we *believe* differently.

I came up with a saying in those early years when I'd end up in a discussion with somebody who was trying to debate and convince me to doubt. When they'd try to "reason with me" and get me to water down my faith, I'd remind them of what God already said in His Word. If they pushed and still tried to teach me to doubt, I'd just say, "Well! *Somebody* is lying . . . I pick you!" I still say that joke today because it works!

You see, I don't care how distinguished or how "good" an argument somebody is making if it's in opposition to Jesus. If they are going against what Jesus said, well, they can keep their opinion—but I'm not taking it. I don't want to learn their doubt. I don't want to be blinded by their unbelief. I want the life God has told me I can have, and I want to live it in childlike faith. So, if someone doesn't feel the same, that's fine—we all choose what we want to do. We can agree to disagree and still enjoy each other's company. But if they want to keep arguing, I can't do that. I just shake the dust off my feet, so to speak, and keep on walking by faith.

God can handle people, and some, I believe, He will have to train in Heaven! To me, there just is no good in arguing with someone who simply does not want to believe.

People Always Ask Me, "Brother Jesse, How'd You Get So Confident?"

People ask me all the time, "How'd you get so confident in yourself?" The truth is that what they think they see is just a side effect of never learning to doubt. You see, I *can't* do any of this on my own. I know it. I'm not that good! So, I'm not confident in myself— but I am very confident in God! I'm confident in *His* ability to use me, teach me, and give me favor wherever I go. I'm *super*-confident in His ability to perform His Word. That is faith. That's all that is!

Think of it like this: When you *know* that the God inside of you is bigger than any challenge, it's easy to look confident. When you know that all things are possible with God, and He called you to do something you *know* you can't do on your own, you just start relying on Him. You have to! If you want to do what He said, you just have to start thinking that with God, you can handle *what-*

ever challenge comes up. So, you take a step forward. Then, you take another.

One step at a time, you move forward. And you don't spin in your head about it because you know that if you could do it on your own, you would. You can't, so you know "I've gotta trust God in this," and you do. Entertaining doubt just multiplies doubt—it adds to confusion and subtracts results. If you want results, you have to *move*. You have to take a step forward. You choose to believe that God is with you because even that's the truth. The truth is, *He* can—and because He's *in* you, He can help you more than you could ever do on your own.

The Dead and the Avoiders Have One Thing in Common: Neither Move

Sometimes doubt hides under procrastination. Avoiding doing something gives some people a false sense of peace. The avoidance becomes a temporary relief of the stress of thinking about actually *doing* something. But let's face it, nobody ever got anywhere by *avoiding* going there!

If you have something God has put on your heart, or something you are believing Him for and you actually want to do it, don't let the stress of overthinking it pile up. Just realize you are avoiding out of doubt and fear. Sometimes just knowing that will help you to see how silly it is to keep avoiding what you actually want to accomplish.

You can't move forward by avoiding. You move forward by taking action. That action may be as simple as praying, it may be confessing the Word, or putting a message on that inspires you. It may be actually taking action in the direction of your dream, or a project, or whatever it is you need to do. Doubt that comes disguised as procrastination is a form of fear for most—it's usually self-doubt. As believers, we conquer self-doubt by realizing we do everything with God.

Some procrastinate because they are waiting to feel like they "are ready"—but if you already know you can't do it on your own, why wait? God is with you; don't doubt that. Nobody who waits until they "feel like it" usually feels like it. Nobody who waits until everything is perfect and they "feel ready" usually feels ready.

God is ready. He's always ready. His Word says that He's called me to be instant in season and out—that means whatever time it is, in season or not, God has called me to live by faith, give of myself, and move forward in my ministry. Whatever I have to do, He's ready to help me do. Step by step, I know that I know that I *know* He will help me finish my course, if I keep the faith.

You see, living by faith isn't *just* about praying and reading the Word; it's about taking action in your own life according to your faith. To live by faith is to take action. Faith without works is dead, and the dead have one thing in common with avoiders: Neither MOVE.

Well, God has called me to move. I'm alive and breathing, so I might as well take action and enjoy this life and the work God has called me to do. Remember that action itself—whatever it is— will help you to break the habit of overthinking. Even if you are not motivated, you can create momentum one step at a time. Every step in faith you take shows you that you "can" because God is with you. Again, this is plain old faith and confidence in God, and it works. It's called never learning to doubt!

People Always Ask Me, "Brother Jesse, How'd You Get So Bold?

People also always ask me, "Brother Jesse, how'd you get so bold? You'll just say anything, and it looks like you don't fear at all." The answer to that is, well, boldness is just a side effect of the Holy Spirit within me. Go and read about the disciples in the Upper Room when the Holy Spirit came down, and you'll see how boldness came into their lives, too.

Those disciples and followers of Jesus were in hiding—they were timid because Jesus had been killed for His beliefs, and they were worried about what might happen to them. They were people like you and me, but many were fearful of the future. They were uncertain about everything because they'd just lost Jesus to the cross and the grave. And even though He had appeared to them after His death and told them to go to the Upper Room and wait, they were still uncertain about their lives. Where would they go? What would they do next?

What happened to them after the Holy Spirit came down in the Upper Room? Boldness! They went from hiding to being seen everywhere. They went from being quiet about Jesus for fear of persecution to going straight out into the streets of Jerusalem to preach the message of Christ. When the Holy Spirit came down and entered them, fear left and boldness took its place. They were in the streets witnessing, telling the stories of Jesus, and getting people saved.

Boldness gave them the guts to preach—and they began Christianity right there on the streets of Jerusalem. They weren't doing all that on their own. They weren't all naturally bold people. They were in fear for their lives just the day before. No, the Holy Spirit within them had infused them with boldness, and they knew they had to speak the truth. In the face of persecution, ridicule, and knowing talking about Jesus could possibly bring them death, they spoke the truth. They lived with boldness. They had confidence in God.

Now, if the early disciples could do *that*, surely we can stop trying to "protect ourselves" from "being disappointed" if we put our faith out there! Surely we can stop avoiding or procrastinating over what God's put on our heart. I rely on the Holy Spirit every day. I stir up the gift of God every day—that means I fellowship with Him every day. I check in with Him in the morning before I check in with anybody or anything. Why? I need to stir up my gift—for that day, for whatever step I will be taking.

I never learned to doubt. I decided to take a simple approach to doing the things I can't do—and that means just accepting that it's God's job to help me do my job. We're in this together, and that is that. It's this kind of mindset that looks at the day in front of me and says, "God will give the strength I need to be 'more than a conqueror' today, to take whatever step I need to take to do His will. I'll overcome whatever may arise and come out better in the end because I have favor and God is with me. If a problem comes, I can change it with my faith, and if I make a mistake, God will correct me and guide me. No devil in hell will stop me. I will accomplish what God has put in front of me today!"

That's what it sounds like in your own head when you choose not to doubt, and I've got to tell you . . . it sounds good to me. Let words like that come out of your mouth in the morning. Make it a habit and you'll see. It's hard to doubt when the Word is going in and coming out of you every day.

Your confidence in God will grow the more you fill up your mind with the Word. You'll become bolder than you once were, too. You'll see more of what you want happen, and you'll see that courage and faith go hand in hand with manifesting God's promises.

Without the blindfold of doubt, life becomes more of an adventure. The days go by quicker because the energy of faith brings you focus and excitement about what comes next. The more you live by faith, the more memories of goals being met, victories being won, and God-touched experiences start stacking up. You start seeing that your life is about using faith to prove to yourself what's possible for you with God—in whatever area you choose to focus on.

The believer's life should be full of experiences worth remembering. Even the hard things, the experiences you wish hadn't come, can end up being something you look at with pride—as in, "Look how God brought me through this! Look what He did with me in this! What the devil meant for harm, God actually turned around for good—because I always believed He would!" What goes well and what doesn't are experiences worth remembering when you see them through the lens of faith.

The believer's life is not supposed to be boring. It can be peaceful and exhilarating at the same time—because peace of mind comes along with the wonder of childlike faith and the experiences that faith creates. Life is better with wonder! It's a key factor to living for the Lord. He enjoys amazing us if we'll have the faith to believe that He can.

I believe that, over and over, as you cast doubt out of your mind, you're going to see God show up and show out in your life. You're going to see His Word come to pass in ways you never thought of as you live by faith. One day, who knows? You just might look back at a great life of faith and have people ask you what they always ask me: "How'd you get so bold and blessed?" Maybe you'll end up saying some version of what I say, too: "It all started when I decided to never learn to doubt God!"

Humanity's Fall Didn't Begin with Sin, It Began with Deliberate Doubt

WHAT STARTED WITH A QUESTION
ENDED WITH AN EXPULSION

When did doubt start on this earth? It began all the way back in the Garden of Eden. In Genesis, we read that everything was perfect when doubt about God's goodness and honesty came in. Nothing was wrong. You see, you can doubt God even when everything is going well. You don't need any trouble or any challenge in order to doubt God. Doubt is an intruder, and the story of Eve and the serpent shows us that doubt always starts the same way—with a question.

Let's read Genesis 3:1-7 now: *"Now the serpent was more subtil than any beast of the field which the Lord God had made. And he said unto the woman, Yea, hath God said, Ye shall not eat of every tree of the garden?"* (vs. 1). Notice the temptation began with a question about what God said. Now, the Word made a point to tell us that the serpent was subtle. In another version, it uses the word "cunning."

Satan threw the question to Eve with seeming innocence. He knew what God had said. He wanted to engage her in conversation, to make a connection and an appeal to her natural senses—to get her mind thinking more like him, against God. The minute that she engaged with the doubt-bringer, Eve was in a battle she didn't even realize she was fighting.

"Yea, hath God said" was nothing more than a way to lure a woman of faith. It was innocent on the surface but evil under-

neath, because the motive of the devil is always to get us to side with him and call God a liar. He wants to hurt the One he rebelled against. He wants to bring us into our own destruction because we are God's own, and we were made in God's image. Of course, the devil can't force us to do anything. We have to agree with him. So, his entry point is always going to be subtle and deceptive because he is cunning.

Don't Let the Conversation Go Too Long—Shut It Down

Eve answered very simply: *"And the woman said unto the serpent, We may eat of the fruit of the trees of the garden: But of the fruit of the tree which is in the midst of the garden, God hath said, Ye shall not eat it, neither shall ye touch it, lest ye die"* (vs. 2-3). Now, she should have stopped right there after she spoke the Word. She didn't have to go any further because what was the point of talking anymore about the tree? Eve said God had already said it was a life or death situation to eat of it or even touch it—and so that should have been the end of it.

Why did the conversation continue? Eve didn't continue it; the serpent did. So, what does this tell us? It tells us that Satan is going to put the pressure on. It means that when he tries to get us to doubt, he is not going to be content with us only saying what God says— he wants to pressure us to engage with him. Eve was engaged in a conversation with the devil at this point, and the problem is that her attention remained on the conversation.

You've got to say no to doubt, push it out, and don't give it the time of day—shut it down before it starts dragging you off course. Yes, doubt about what God said in His Word may enter your mind, but it's what you *do* with that thought once it comes that matters. Do not let yourself be lured in. That was Eve's problem. She listened too long and got lured in. She should have shut it down right after she said what God said, but she didn't.

What Begins as a Question Turns to an Attack on God

The conversation went on: *"And the serpent said unto the woman, Ye shall not surely die: For God doth know that in the day ye eat thereof, then your eyes shall be opened, and ye shall be as gods, knowing good and evil"* (vs. 4-5). Satan shows his true colors right here. He's not subtle anymore—he cannot help speaking directly against God Almighty.

Satan hates God. He hates us because God loves us. His subtlety will always shift into an outright verbal attack on God because he cannot contain his hatred for God and the Word of God. It will come out. You see, doubt starts with a question and moves to an attack on God's character. Notice that the serpent immediately calls God Almighty a liar: *"Ye shall not surely die."* Then, he tells her a lie! Notice Satan accuses God of being what *he* is! This is how most manipulators work because they are playing by the handbook of the original manipulator.

Satan starts spinning a tale right here. When he begins his lie with *"For God doth know,"* he is again saying God is a liar. That's twice. First he says it directly with *"Ye shall not surely die"* and again when he begins deception with *"For God doth know."* In other words, "Eve, God knows that what I'm about to tell you is the real truth. *God* is just a liar who doesn't want the best for you . . . but *I* do. I'm going to let you in on a secret about that tree."

Satan will always do this kind of thing. He'll even pull the name of God into his lies, if you give him time to talk. He will make it seem that God is distant and that he is right there with you, that he's the one who's really got your back, and that he's going to illuminate your mind with something truer than God.

The Appeal of the Deception

It's all manipulation. It's all a lie. But it will *still* be appealing, make no mistake—because the longer you listen to the doubt-bringer, the more he'll try to tempt you to side with him instead of with God. He'll offer you what you may long to have. Or he may offer you what you never knew you always wanted . . . until you heard it!

When he told Eve, *"your eyes shall be opened,"* he was tempting her by appealing to her desire for full vision and full clarity about how the world worked. Now, God wanted her to have faith in Him, to live free and childlike in paradise with no needs, and everything she could want easily accessible and at her fingertips. It was perfect already, remember that. Satan was saying, "You don't need faith in God—He's deceiving you anyway. Just disobey Him and see. Let *me* show you how to open your eyes so you can see all the good and all the evil there is to see . . . like God can . . . like I can. Don't you want to see? Don't you want to be like us gods? Let me show you everything. Don't you want to know?"

When the serpent told Eve that she could *"be as gods, knowing good and evil,"* he wasn't just tempting Eve with something random—he was revealing his own desire to remake Adam and Eve in his *own* image. Notice he didn't say she'd be like God. He said she'd be like "gods"—which is what the devil considered himself, even in that serpent form. He was trying to get Eve to make his will her will, to make his desires her desires. He was trying to damage God's beloved creation by stealing the innocence God had given them and told them to protect. You could even say that he was trying to recreate his own fall from Heaven, through mankind, right here on the earth by getting God's beloved creation to revolt. Never forget that the devil is a fallen angel who thinks and will always portray himself as an enlightener of humanity.

Doubt Is a Liar—It Poses as Rational and Truthful

Now, let's back up and remember that Eve already had been given the truth. She was living better than any woman has ever lived on this planet. And even in that blessed state, she fell into the lies. Doubt is a liar because it began with the author of lies. Remember that Satan convinced a third of Heaven to fall when he rebelled against God—and it was even more perfect in Heaven, and yet still they were swayed.

Sometimes we can have everything we need and want and still doubt God's goodness and honesty. We can have everything we desire even and still doubt His intentions. Doubt is not rational, but it poses as rational. It's not truthful, but it poses as a form of truth. It is an invader. And unless we protect ourselves by stopping it quickly and choosing God's Word over the temptation to side with the devil in order to be *"as gods,"* we will fall, just like the third of Heaven and just like Adam and Eve. Remember that you can't fall if you don't listen to the lies of the devil. You won't be lured if you stop the conversation short and don't entertain the opposition. When God said not to put any gods before Him, He was trying to protect us from falling into the trap of deceitful demonic liars who call themselves "gods" and have posed as enlighteners of mankind for millennia.

You see, the devil is *going* to weave a web of deception—that's what he does, and when he's talking to a person of faith, he will always use doubt about God's nature or intent to do it. It's what he does. He's a liar. We learn from Eve's mistake that entertaining the doubt-bringer and pondering the doubtful words too long lessens the odds we'll get out alive.

The Word is our final authority as believers—and once we start being wishy-washy about what God said, engaging in ideas that what He said isn't true, we are just aligning ourselves with the original accuser of God: Satan. That may seem strong, but it really is either faith or sin. That's what the Word says in Romans 14:23, so don't think that doubt is a minor player. It's a key player!

When we allow doubt to ramble on and remain, when we allow it to basically call God a liar in our own mind, it may not seem to be killing us, but it is. It will kill our dreams, our hopes, our peace, and our joy. It is a tragedy. Losing out on God's best is exactly that to me, a tragedy. It's a fall from where we were always meant to be—which is with God, living on the side of right and truth, subduing the evil that comes up with God's Word, and going on to enjoy the good life He's always wanted us to have.

Doubt Was the First Theft of Man's Position

"And when the woman saw that the tree was good for food, and that it was pleasant to the eyes, and a tree to be desired to make one wise, she took of the fruit thereof, and did eat, and gave also unto her husband with her; and he did eat. And the eyes of them both were opened, and they knew that they were naked; and they sewed fig leaves together, and made themselves aprons" (vs. 6-7).

Eve chose her senses over God. Eve chose her curiosity over God. She wouldn't have talked to the serpent if she weren't interested in what he had to say. She wouldn't have looked at the tree if she hadn't started to believe the serpent's lies.

Once she listened too long, she started to look. Once she looked, she started to desire. It was pleasant to her eyes—because now, it didn't look like the tree God had said not to eat from. She was seeing the tree through the lens of deception. It looked like wisdom to her. It looked like equality with God.

Once that prideful desire pulled on her, she didn't hesitate— she took of the tree and she ate, and once she ate, she didn't want to eat alone. You see, doubt is easily shared, and it always multiplies. These are lessons we can take away to help us to stop playing with the lies before they lead us down the wrong path. Eve gave the fruit to her husband, and notice that he didn't reject it— he could have but didn't. He ate it. In other words, Adam chose his mate over his God and with that, with two in agreement, they made a combined choice.

Their combined choice showed that they were actively rejecting God as the truthful Creator—and choosing the serpent as their liberator. They were showing that they cared more about their own bellies and their own desires for power than they cared about their Father God.

Were their eyes opened like the serpent said? Yes, in a way, because Satan always weaves an element of truth into his lies—but they did not get the wisdom he promised, and they did not become anywhere near "like God." They got exactly what God said they'd get if they disobeyed and ate: death.

Death of the Good Life and the Birth of Newfound Shame

Death came, make no mistake. There was no such thing as death before, but their bodies began degenerating then, and physical death would eventually come—but not before they experienced a whole range of other deaths. Death of the blessing on their lives. Death of the abundance they once knew in every way. Death of the childlike freedom of living in paradise, where everything was easy. Death of the intimate relationship they once shared with God Himself. Expulsion was coming.

With their chosen rebellion against God came not only the death of the good life they had before, but the birth of a newfound shame—a humiliating and desperate need to be covered up. Satan's lie had led them to that, stripped of God's glory and stripped of all dignity. You see, they knew that they were naked and not just on their flesh, but something had shifted in their spirit. Stripped bare of God's glory and His best for their lives, they went scrambling around looking for a substitute.

People are still looking for a substitute today, and I'm not talking about clothes. Even today, when people are in rebellion against God, they will look for a substitute—and this includes believers who choose to say they believe God but actively doubt His love, concern, power, and will to do what He has said in His Word.

We were created to be clothed in His glory—to live in a spiritual state of being that is at one with our Father God. That's God's best for us. If we want to stay on the path of His best, we have to take doubting God seriously. We can't downplay it. To stay on the path of God's best requires that we actively condition ourselves to make the right choice when confronted with doubtful thoughts, doubt-loving people, and even spiritual hammering from God's enemies—and do it quickly.

Doubt Started as a Suggestion, and That Suggestion Led to an Expulsion

Doubt suggests you question God's goodness. Doubt suggests you weigh God's motives. Doubt tries to put you in the driver's seat, as if you are the Creator and God is the creation. It's an inversion of truth and a twisting of reality. What started as a suggestion in the Garden led to an expulsion—it took two people right out of the place they wanted to be. Doubt can change your location from where you should be to where you were never meant to be. Like sin, it can lead you to a place in life that you never thought you'd end up—because the choice to doubt is a choice to walk away from God's best. The problem that led to the Fall was doubt—because sin may have taken them out of the garden, but doubt is what got the ball rolling.

Not only did Adam and Eve's location change, but their clothes changed, too. Before doubt and sin, the first man and woman were clothed with righteousness and glory. Once stripped of righteousness and glory, they were truly naked. This wasn't just bare skin; this was a bare soul. What was once filling their heart and surrounding their flesh was suddenly gone, and they felt the loss. That loss came with shame. Why? Because man was never meant to be bare-souled! That "nakedness" is an empty feeling, and it was a brand-new feeling for Adam and Eve. It was yet another form of death, and again, they felt the loss and immediately tried to hide.

What did man and woman do when they lost the glory of God? They looked for a substitute—anything they could get to cover up the vulnerability of being suddenly without God's glory. What was once full circle around them, inside and out, left what you could call a wound—they were suddenly exposed and "knew" they were naked. Immediately, something had to die. Animal skins became their clothing to cover their exposed flesh, and soon, animal sacrifice would come as well to cover their sin for a time.

Now, before that, animals were free and not used to fulfill man's inadequacies or appetites. But in a sin-state, something has to die for something else to live. Sin is a debt. If you don't think God counts the animals He made as precious and even holy in His sight, then you haven't considered that animal sacrifice was the precursor for God's only begotten Son's sacrifice for all of mankind. Their lives are worth something precious to God—so much so that their sacrifice in Old Testament times had the power to cover the sins of people. Think about that!

We call Jesus the Ultimate Sacrifice because His one sacrifice paid the price for all people—past, present, and future. No longer did the animals have to suffer. No longer did mankind just have atonement. You see, unlike every other sacrifice made to temporarily atone for sin, Jesus' sacrifice was a forever work. His blood doesn't cover sin; His blood washes sin away, never to be remembered against the transgressor any more. The work Jesus did for mankind on the cross is the only acceptable sacrifice for sin, according to God. This is why when we call on the name of Jesus, when we ask for forgiveness, there is nothing more we have to do to handle our transgressions—because His blood has already done it, and done it all.

Jesus is our covering. Jesus fills the spiritual space that Adam and Even lost when they doubted God and chose sin. This is why people often feel so light and free when they get saved and ask for forgiveness from God. The Holy Spirit comes to live in the naked place of the soul—filling the soul with the Spirit of God, shedding the love of God abroad in the heart, and giving man a new start without the weight of sin.

What tempts a man or a woman is always in the sensory realm—we're all tempted by what we see, smell, hear, taste, or touch. So, remember that Satan will always pull on you in those areas. The tree of the knowledge of good and evil was beautiful like everything God creates, but it wasn't until the serpent pointed it out and Eve gazed at it longingly that she made the decision that it looked good to eat.

Why didn't they just eat of the tree of life? God had placed it in the garden, too. The Word says the same tree is in Heaven as well. The fruit and the leaves are not symbolic, but a tangible creation of God that brings life. Life was in the Garden. The knowledge of good and evil was in the Garden, too.

Sometimes we have choices and it's obvious which one is better. The wise recognize when they are being pulled away by the subtle assault of temptation. Those who pause and realize that their senses are being used against them have the advantage—because time is important when dealing with temptation. How long you contemplate the wrong matters. The "power of pause" is taking that breath and pausing in the moment of temptation to realize your senses are about to take you for a ride!

Once sin came in, destruction followed. Sin is fun for a time, but it's never fun in the end. The truth is that the tree of life was always more powerful than the tree of the knowledge of good and evil. What looked tempting to them paled in comparison to what they already had.

Have you ever seen someone throw away a good life for a temporary high? People look back with regret when they give up so much to get so little. From the beginning of time until now, people are searching for the fountain of youth. They fantasize about immortality, about abundance, about beauty, and about living in a state of blissful ease and youth. In other words, mankind has been aching to get back what they lost when they decided they wanted to know what evil was like—when they decided God didn't have their best interests at heart.

Well, we've got knowledge now! Since the knowledge of good and evil showed up, are we any happier, freer, or better? No. Because just like everything else God says, He was right in the first place! We're living in a fallen world now, and only those that have gotten so accustomed to acting evil enjoy it when evil runs amuck in the world—but even they are just deceived and can be saved if they open their eyes to the truth and turn to God. Remember that the worst of offenders against God and against good are not hopeless. *All* can be saved. *All* can be forgiven. *All* can have the nakedness of their soul—the one they try to fill up with all sorts of other things to replace the need for God—filled with the Holy Spirit!

The promises of God are far more powerful than the sins of people. There is no sin too great that the blood of Jesus can't wash it away. My mother was born again, and God's promise to her was far more powerful than my sins—and I was a serious sinner. I loved sin. I didn't even think about God. Yet God was thinking about me! Mama was thinking about me too, and praying for me diligently. My wife, Cathy, says that I was such a terrible sinner that God had to give Jesus a blood transfusion just to make up for His loss! That's a joke, but you get the idea.

What You Don't Subdue May Cause You to Submit

There are so many lessons that could be taught about how deception won in the Garden, but I hope that you will see that time itself is important in giving you the resisting edge. When doubt shows up, and it will, don't entertain it, don't rehearse it, and don't let the devil lie to you about anything God says is right, wrong, or otherwise.

The Word tells us as believers to be as wise as serpents and as harmless as doves for a reason—because godly wisdom, which is founded on spiritual truth and a deep reverence and respect for

God, can easily conquer satanic manipulation . . . but only if we wise up. There's too much at stake *not* to nip it in the bud quickly.

If we do not subdue doubt in our own lives when it rises, it will run roughshod right over us—what we don't subdue may end up causing us to submit. Remember that the command to be fruitful, multiply, replenish the earth, and subdue in Genesis 1:28 was given *before* the serpent ever showed up. So, we *still* need to rule our own lives with this command in mind so we don't get waylaid.

There are many lies of the enemy vying for our attention today. There are the dictates of our own flesh and the unrenewed thoughts of our mind to contend with, too. But we can stay on the right path if we have the wisdom to make God's Word the last word for us— and this is a choice we make both when everything's perfect and when nothing seems to be going right. Doubt doesn't care either way; it'll still try to steal from you in good times or in bad. But God's truth will guide you and keep you on the right track if you choose to let it be your final authority.

Remember that the wrong paths in life are filled with cultivated doubt about God and ourselves—and those doubts arise subtly but quickly turn to an attack against God's truth. Never forget that the longer you listen to and cultivate doubt, the harder it will be to resist lies. Lies will start sounding better to you than the truth. Don't let that happen. Take the Garden as a lesson and realize that what began with a question led to an expulsion, and it's a cautionary lesson about how following lies leads to misery.

Time can be on your side or the serpent's side—you can let doubt keep talking or you can shut it down quickly. Choose instead to just speak the Word and turn away from anything that rises up and shows itself against God and His best plan for your life. Be on the side of what's right. Remember that whatever doesn't lead you toward God and what's good is probably trying to steer you where you really do not want to be.

Be on the side of truth no matter what cunning and subtle enemy tries to sway you into lies. It's a choice you make in the moment to be who God said you could be and have what God said you could have. I pray you decide to shut doubt down every time it tries to lure you. I pray you simply make the choice to believe. I pray you let the story of the Fall be a reminder to you that doubting God is always a mistake—you'll always give up more than you get in return when you choose a lie over the truth of God's Word.

I hope that when temptation to doubt God comes (and it will), you'll say "no" and just side with God no matter what! After all, there's just no good reason to give up a whole Garden of "good" in exchange for one lousy, stinking piece of tempting fruit.

Goals, Manifestations, and Surprises from God

NEVER LEARNING TO DOUBT IS A LIFESTYLE OF TRUST

I f you are a believer, then believe. You'll see that the simple act of believing changes the energy inside of you and around you, too. You see things differently. You perceive even problems through the lens of a belief that is assured that God is on your side—and that means you are going to not just be OK, but you are going to be great!

My life today is better than I even imagined when I first said, "God, come into my life." Never learning to doubt means my "salvation" isn't just some lofty idea. I didn't choose Christianity because it had a good code of ethics; I chose it because Jesus first chose me, and He has the words of life. It's not just a bunch of nice sounding words; it's the words of *life*. Never learning to doubt means I've decided to believe that I'm on God's side and He's on mine.

The blood of Jesus saved my soul, and His principles saved my way of life. No matter what the enemy throws at me, I never learned to doubt that with God, I'm going to overcome. God's plan for my life *will* come to pass. Every day, I teach myself not to doubt by reading God's Word, confessing its truth over my life, and fellowshipping daily with the Lord Jesus. This relationship I've cultivated makes it hard *not* to follow the Holy Spirit's leading—I know He's there, so I'm not going to deliberately disobey Him.

Having His Word in me means it comes up in my mind in tough times; so I have something to pull on when circumstances come up. Living like this on a daily basis—not a Sunday basis—makes it hard for me *not* to have faith in God. I don't go by what I see. I go by what I believe. And my faith creates the changes I want, sometimes quickly and sometimes in time, but none of that matters because I know it's going to happen if I don't get weary in well-doing.

Let the Lord Interrupt Your Plans—You Never Know Who Is on the Other Side of Your Obedience

I don't just randomly make plans with my life—I seek the Lord to see what He would have me to do. Sometimes He tells me straightforwardly and guides me by giving me a vision of tomorrow ahead of time. Sometimes He doesn't do that at all. Sometimes He just guides me one step at a time.

I love living for the Lord because it's an adventure. What am I going to do today? I already have a schedule, of course, but the Lord knows that if He interrupts it, I'll listen and go whatever way He is leading me that day. No matter what I aim to do, I want to be guided by the Holy Spirit—and if that means a detour in my plans, guess what? I'm taking the detour!

My mother was a woman who followed the Holy Spirit's leading, too. She's in Heaven now, but when I was young, I remember how the Holy Spirit prompted her to get up, get in her truck, and go to the levee. She wasn't planning to go there before. She had other plans for the day. But, as the Word says in Proverbs 16:9, a man makes his plans, but it is the Lord who orders his steps (man means mankind there, of course). My mother was very sensitive to the Holy Spirit and listened to that prompting, even though she had no idea what she'd find. That day, the Lord led her to a girl standing on the levee of the Mississippi River who was about to commit suicide by jumping in and drowning herself.

The girl was pregnant, didn't want to tell her parents, and had come to the end of her rope. She was distraught, crying hard, and just about to jump when my mother showed up. Mama was able to talk to her, share words of hope with her, and the girl listened—and she invited Jesus into her life. My mother said afterward that she wondered what would have happened if she'd hesitated in listening to the Lord, or if she'd ignored Him altogether?

Now, I was young, but my mother's obedience to the leading of the Holy Spirit affected me. Even when I wasn't serving the Lord, I knew that those who were sensitive could be given messages that, if they listened, led them to help others or avoid trouble for themselves. I'd seen and heard too much to deny it, even if I didn't want to talk about it back then.

I met that girl years later at a tent revival meeting that I preached. She'd grown into a woman with a family of her own. She told me she credited my mama for saving her life. The reality was that Mama was just an obedient believer, but *God* was the One that saved her life. My mother was just sensitive to His voice and obedient enough to follow His lead.

You see, the wonderful thing about following the Holy Spirit inside of you, even with a bunch of doubt clogging up your spiritual ears, is that you can still be led to help others in ways you may not even realize are important. Maybe it won't be as dramatic as saving a girl on a levee about to commit suicide, or maybe it will be even more dramatic than that. The Lord works in mysterious ways, but only those who believe, listen, and obey can more quickly be guided by His voice.

When you live a never-learned-to-doubt kind of life, you may or may not realize *who* you have affected for good. You may or may not realize *what* bad things in life you have avoided by being sensitive, willing, and obedient either. Until you get to Heaven, you may not even see the fruit of your sensitivity-seeds, but that is not what matters. All that matters is that you didn't doubt, that you listened, and that you walked by faith.

I Don't Believe You Have to "See" Everything You Dream or Desire Before It Manifests

Sometimes the Lord will give you a vision or goal to aim toward. Sometimes the Lord will surprise you instead. Either way, if you're living a never-learned-to-doubt kind of life, you're trusting that step-by-step, He will be faithful to bring you where you need to be—and if the devil fights you, God will give you the wisdom, strength, and joy to overcome it and have a testimony on the other end. As they say, you can't have a testimony until you have a test. The test isn't the problem though. The test is what you do when faced with that problem. Will you have faith in God, will you apply His Word, and will you confess it and act in wisdom upon it? That's the test!

Never learning to doubt is a lifestyle of trust. I trust that God is guiding me every day. I put Him first, and I know He's going to put me first, too. He loves me, and I love Him, and He's helping me as I move through this life. Some people believe you have to *see* every single thing you dream or desire inside your mind's eye before it manifests in your life, but I don't believe that's always the case.

I believe in having goals and dreams, seeing them, and calling those things that be not as though they were like Romans 4:17 says. I believe in having a plan. I believe in manifesting whatever God puts on my heart as a desire. But I also believe that sometimes God likes to surprise me. I believe that God is always guiding me. I trust in His goodness toward me. Because of that, I know that He is going to bless me with even what I can't or don't "see" in my mind's eye of faith. I believe He is propelling me to where I'm meant to be in life. I believe if you put Him first, He'll do the same for you—and some of those "meant to be" people/places/things in your life will be a surprise blessing you never saw coming.

Trusting God and the things He's said in the Word is a foundational principle for being a believer. Making Him first in our life keeps us in sync with Him so He can guide us more easily. Making His Word a priority gives us the foundation we need to be instant in season and out, and spiritually ready for anything—which not only gives us something to pull on during challenging times and keeps us on the straight path of righteousness, but it also makes us a quick encourager to others. When we trust Him with our own path, He'll draw others to us who need the wisdom of the Word in their situations, too.

Believers Work in Two Dimensions— We're in This World, but We're Not of This World

You are a spirit being, you're eternal, and this life is a vapor—it goes as fast as hair spray flying out the can! Pfffffft . . . vapor! The real you inside that body is hooked up to God, and the closer you get to God and not doubting Him, the more you'll know how He guides you in life. The more you'll marvel at the steps He's guided you to take.

God's Word is the only thing that will last in the end, so don't just read it—believe it. I often say, if you don't learn it here, you'll have to learn it in Heaven. We will keep learning even after earthly death because we were created to learn and grow. Our bodies will one day be incorruptible, but that doesn't mean we will stop exploring and growing in the knowledge of who God is and what He has created. Science has touched the tip of the iceberg when it comes to the things and places God has made. I love science and hearing their theories, but one day we won't have to wonder which theory is correct—because we will be in the direct presence of the Maker of all things.

Something can't come from nothing, but nothing can come from Something. God is God, and He can create or lay it to waste. I love when Jesus was teaching in John 10:18 and started talking about His own life, saying, *"No man taketh it from Me, but I lay it down of Myself. I have power to lay it down, and I have power to take it again. This commandment have I received of My Father."* Whoa! In other words, Jesus wanted everyone that day to know that *nobody* had the power to take His life from Him, and yet He *allowed* Himself to be crucified for us because He knew it was better for *us*. That's love. That's true power in action. God is merciful and gracious. He's not looking to hurt us; He's looking to help us—but we must help ourselves and believe Him. We take the Word into our own mouth. We open our eyes to the truth. We act on what we know and move forward in faith, trusting that the Holy Spirit will lead us in all things.

The heavens and the earth will pass away one day, but God's words will never pass away (Matthew 24:35). What He says sticks! He is the Author and Finisher of our faith. So, why would any believer want to doubt God? Why would we doubt what is eternal and instead put faith in what we can temporarily see? Do we think our eyes will outlast God? Do we think anything will outlast God?

I've read the back of the Book, and guess what? In the end, we win—no matter how much God's adversary tries to convince mankind otherwise. He's a twister of truth. He's a liar and a thief. Don't let the faith in your heart be something he robs, too. Doubt is a losing mindset. Being a never-learned-to-doubt kind of believer means not accepting a losing mindset in this temporary life—it means adopting the eternal mindset of winning.

There is no sickness, poverty, or misery in Heaven because it's not God's will for Heaven. Jesus told us in Matthew 6:10 to pray that God's will be done here, *"as it is in Heaven."* He taught that faith is what makes us whole, faith is what provides needs and desires, and faith is what is required to ask *anything* in His name and see it done (Matthew 9:22; Mark 11:22-24; John 14:13-14). You see, when your heart is right, you don't have to worry about greed and envy because those things don't fit in a mind that is renewed to the Word and a heart that is filled with the Holy Spirit. I wrote in more detail about this in my last book, *Your Everything Is Anything*, so I won't go into it further, but I hope you understand! I make no excuses for the blessings of God on my life, and I refuse to bow down to the status quo of doubt that has become the religious world.

I'm in this world but not *of* this world, and you are too. You see, we are products of two different dimensions of life that we know about, and both are running parallel to each other—the natural world we see and the spirit world that we don't see, unless God pulls back the veil. From time to time, He does pull back that veil! But, as Jesus said, it's better for us if we believe and don't see.

Why is it better for us to have faith and not just lean on our eyes? It's better because the energy behind faith works when we *use* it—again, it's an energy force. Seeing does not create change. Faith creates change. It is by faith and not by sight that we move things in both dimensions. This is how God made the two dimensions to work together.

The angels see our faith and hear our words, too—both holy angels and fallen angels. This means that God's angels work with us if we are using faith and God's Words. It also means that demons know when we are using our faith and God's Words, which is the sword of the Spirit (Ephesians 6:17). What you believe matters, not just what you say. When what you believe and what you say match the Word, you are powerful in two places—the natural world and the spirit world.

My Wait Time Isn't My Worry Time
Because I Trust God All the Time

Anything that pertains to life and godliness is for you, if you've got the desire to believe for it (2 Peter 1:3-4). Whether it's spiritual, physical, or financial, you can put your faith and words toward it and see results. If you don't give up, if you don't get weary, you can enforce the devil's defeat and draw God's blessings into your life in whatever area you desire. It's called manifesting your desires, and it's not a secular mindset—it's a faith principle that was taught by Jesus Christ.

A lot of people worry about the "time" when they are praying and believing for something specific. They forget that only this natural world works according to the sun. That's man's way of telling "time." God doesn't need to "tell time" because He works outside of time, which means that when we are praying for something, we're talking to the One Who created time—and the One Who's perspective we need to gain more than our own.

A lot of people give up when they don't see manifestation fast enough. I do the opposite. When I feel a tinge of discontent about the time factor, I increase my faith. When it looks like nothing is happening or the devil is fighting to hinder my manifestation, I put the force of faith into effect even more.

Every time it comes up in my mind, I speak the Word, I call in my manifestation, I rebuke the devil, and I speak by faith *as if* it has already happened. Hebrews 11:1 says, *"Now faith is the substance of things hoped for, the evidence of things not seen"*—so my evidence is what I can't yet see, and that's how I know I've got it. It's a mind-bend, I know! It's not a natural man's way of thinking—the Word is spirit and truth, and when I use it, I know I'm using the words of the other dimension.

The spirit world will affect my natural world if I don't give up—if I put the pressure on my faith, I will see my manifestation. I don't bend to the pressure of time. I remind myself that it's just the sun and nothing more, that I am eternal, and I'm working a divine principle. This line of thinking and acting has always been what moved me from "I believe it" into "I manifested it." I just refuse to be defeated by time, that thing we decided to create because we looked up at the sun! I'm looking at God, the One Who made the sun. If He wants to stop the sun, He can. So, I don't let the wait time become the worry time. That's fear, and I'm not doing that.

You see, your wait time isn't supposed to be your worry time. Worry is a form of fear that God can help you with if you trust Him. Trust cancels out worry. I've decided that this is the day the Lord has made—I might as well *rejoice* and be *glad* for today, because this is the time I've got right now. I trust God with today just like I trust Him with my future.

When you trust, it's easy to have joy in the waiting time. Your mind may want to get you to dive into worrying about time, but take control over that and focus on joy for today. Remind yourself that joy is always available and time is not your enemy. Faith and patience work together to receive the promises of God, according to the Word (Hebrews 6:12). While we may not like that, it's a fact because it's what God said—and you are actually learning as you are exercising faith and patience.

Don't mistake giving up for patience, because patience isn't giving up and doing nothing. Patience is a fruit of the Spirit. So, if you need more, pray for more of God's Spirit to flow through you so that you can live with joy—and not just when you manifest whatever you're believing for, but in the process of believing by faith, too.

I've decided that if I'm an eternal being, then whatever I don't get here, I'll get there—but I know that nine times out of ten, I'll get what I'm believing for here, too, if I just don't give up. I've seen it happen too many times for me to be convinced of anything else. I've convinced myself that God can't lie. So, I don't have a "time problem"—I have an "eternal solution." I know that I can live with both a present joy and a long view perspective.

I encourage you to trust God with today. Have patience *and* faith for what you are believing for tomorrow. Know that those two work in tandem. They are what I always use to pull the manifestation of my prayers into my life, and I know that as you trust God, you can use them successfully, too. Remember that what you start in the spirit shows up in the natural. If you don't give up and never learn to doubt, it has no other choice!

Joy, No Matter What

WHAT I DO WHEN I'M HIT WITH TROUBLE

Have you ever woken up one day and had Good Morning America verbally attacking you? How about Fox News, ABC, CBS, or NBC? I have, and guess what? I'm still smiling! I'm still singing God's praise and still preaching His Word—I'm still giving, receiving, showing love, and living by faith. I don't stop having faith just because I'm being attacked. No, in fact, I lean more on my faith then—I pull on the power of believing, and it doesn't just sustain me so I can "make it" through the hard times; it gives me joy and strength to sail through the hard times! Only the believing life can do that.

My daughter was taken aback by the lies and told me that she was shocked at how well I was handling it. She said, "Daddy, you are the strongest man . . . I don't think I could do it." I said, "Well, Jodi, I already asked the Lord how to handle this. Should I defend myself? Should I fight back or sue those suckers? There are many options for how to handle these kinds of things. I want to 'make them an offer they can't refuse', like *The Godfather* movie! But that's not what God told me to do. He told me to stick with the Book—He gave me 'the joy of the Lord is your strength' scripture and told me I would kill it with joy." So, that's what I did.

I decided not let the attacks steal my joy—and I decided that when it came up, whether in my own mind all alone or in the presence of media asking me questions, I would let the joy of the Lord out. Joy would be my strength. Joy would be my weapon. Joy would be my way of not slipping into doubt, fear, or anything like that. JOY would win.

Now, before I talked to God about it and got that guidance, my natural mind wanted payback. My natural mind wanted to kill them with lawsuits first, and I even caught myself fantasizing about taking them out old mafia-movie style. I had to watch my mind! My mind wanted to stir me up and get me into strife. Of course, I knew I was a "new creature in Christ" because of my salvation, but my mind wanted me to raise up the "old creature" I was before I got saved! It's just a fact that when under pressure, the mind will try to take you back in time. But that's the flesh, and no matter how long you've known the Lord, it's just something you have to deal with.

My flesh wanted to think up a few fantasies about taking my attackers out with a quick *boom boom*, as if I was in the movies. My fleshly mind imagined somebody telling me, "Well, you'll go to jail for the rest of your life," and my fleshly mind imagined answering that with, "Yeah, but you won't be at the trial!" But once I consulted God, I made the decision to follow Him and not my flesh. The flesh leads to nothing good. What feels good for a moment can make a mess out of life.

You've got to take control when your mind is going wild—and you do that by leaning on God, the One Who can handle it better than you! In my situation, after I consulted God, the "persecution" I felt started to seem small. Even if I was being mocked, it was nothing. Even if they cut my guts out with malicious and sensationalized lies, it became nothing. No matter what they said about me and how many friends thought the bad press would ruin my ministry, I kept my joy. And when I looked at it in light of the Word, it wasn't a fraction of the true persecution that the disciples of Christ withstood—not even close!

Mental Anemia Can't Take the Pressure— An Apathetic Mind Runs When Hit with Persecution

Making doubt in God's Word and His power a habit will drain you of the life-sustaining faith you need in the heat of trouble. I call it mental anemia, and those who live that way can't handle the pressure of persecution. A mind that's accustomed to apathy will run in the face of persecution—because the passion they lack in everyday life also steals the passion to rise up with hope. A person living a stagnant-believer's-life will cave to the pressures of this world because they don't have anything to draw from. What you put in will come out. What you choose to think and believe in the easy times affects what you will pull from in the hard times.

You see, I've made up my mind that I decide how I'm going to feel—not the circumstances. I decide what my attitude will be, and I decide I'm going to obey what God tells me over what people tell me. People can't save me. People can't change me. Only God has the power to do either of those, and if I allow Him to lead me, He will always lead me to what is right.

Vengeance is the Lord's, according to the Word—and that means vengeance is not mine! I don't have to like that, but I choose to obey that because I know it's right whether it "feels good" or not. "Feels good" isn't my motivation; faith that God's direction is higher and better than my natural flesh is my motivation. God can turn around situations that look like they're going to ruin you if you follow His lead instead of your own flesh. I chose joy. I responded to attacks from my heart and my mind with joy. I didn't hide out but just kept going about my Father's business—and I hit that situation head-on everywhere I went.

I didn't skirt the issue. I told people the truth about my ministry, and I tried to understand the pressure of the media to get ratings, too. I knew people were going to think what they wanted anyway, so I let them! I didn't try to control it all. I can't tell you how many preachers told me I was finished. I decided to have faith in God—He started it, and He will finish it when He's ready! God is not listening to doubtful people. He chooses what He's going to do, and He told me to have joy.

You Can't Fight Strife with More Strife—
As a Believer, You Fight Your Battles with the Light of God

So, I just decided to have joy in the midst of trouble, and do you know what? It didn't take long for me to see the results of deciding that God's direction was the right direction. Not only was my soul at peace, but the ministry itself *grew*. We grew more that year than any year previous! That's a miracle I couldn't have predicted and I wouldn't have experienced if I had chosen to be led by my fleshly feelings.

Feelings can get you in trouble if you let them take the wheel—they can drive your mind and life right into a ditch! You can't fight darkness with more darkness. You can't fight strife with more strife. You fight all of that with light. In the light of God, there are many emotions to pull from that won't land you in the ditch but will sustain you during tough times. During that time, He led me to focus on joy. You may find He leads you to lean and focus on His love, or His peace, or His long-suffering patience. An anemic mind can be jumpstarted by choosing to follow God's lead instead of the lead of the flesh.

Sometimes, when your flesh is waging a battle for your mind, you just have to make it simple and make a decision to rejoice. Praise has a flesh-busting effect, especially when you do it when nothing in life seems worthy of praise.

I like Philippians 4:4-7, which says, *"Rejoice in the Lord alway: and again I say, Rejoice. Let your moderation be known unto all men. The Lord is at hand. Be careful for nothing; but in every thing by prayer and supplication with thanksgiving let your requests be made known unto God. And the peace of God, which passeth all understanding, shall keep your hearts and minds through Christ Jesus."*

Notice how that instruction tells you that if you begin with joy, you'll end with peace. It will be the type of peace that is beyond understanding. It'll keep (guard) your heart *and* mind through Christ Jesus. I also want you to notice that your prayers and supplications are wedged between the joy and the peace, and they must be mixed with gratitude. That's not about thanking God for the problem but having faith that He is the One Who will lead you to the solution—but first you have to rejoice. I know it's not easy if your emotions are going haywire, but it's an act of obedience. Do it and it will help you to humble yourself before Him, because it's an act of faith in His power to change you. Joy is powerful.

Nobody but me could understand how I could be at peace during that media conflict. That's alright. Nobody needed to understand but me! I'm telling you that the only reason I could have peace is because I followed God's leading and His Word to rejoice first. I rejoiced during the hard time and every time the hard time tried to rise up in my mind. And every time, it brought me peace.

Joy didn't just clear my emotions or my mindset; it helped me act moderately—instead of flying off the handle at people, I was able to glide through trouble and speak my heart without the natural human response of anger at being misrepresented and hurt at being mocked. Never doubt that if you do what God says with a sincere heart, He will fulfill His promise to you. The peace you receive from God during trying times may be beyond understanding to others, but it will guard your heart like nothing else.

What Does Jesus' "Overcoming the World" Have to Do with Me?

Remember, trouble in this life is completely normal. So, like 1 Peter 4:12-13 says, don't think something strange has happened if you experience trials and trouble as a believer. Nobody likes trouble, but it's a fact of life in this fallen, sin-sick world.

Do I have problems that I wish were solved today? Yes! Does the unexpected happen in my life? You better believe it! Have I had opportunities to give up and turn my back on what God has said? Absolutely. I'm living in the world just like you are, but I know that Jesus said in this world I'd have some tribulation. So, then I know that trouble is par for the course. It is just the way it is. But, I also know how He told me to respond to trouble—Jesus taught that I should *"be of good cheer"* knowing *He* has *"overcome the world"* (John 16:33).

You might think, *What does that have to do with me. I know Jesus overcame, but I need to overcome this thing!* When Jesus said to be of good cheer because He overcame the world, He was letting you know that your perspective needs to shift to the spiritual reality when you are dealing with a natural problem—and that cheer or joy itself will break the power of what's attacking you.

Joy will break the problem inside your heart and mind before it ever does anything outside of you. Joy will remove the frustration of the problem because they just can't coexist. The problem will lose its power over your mood and disposition. When you laugh in the face of it, it's like the devil himself can't understand—because as a flesh devil, the joy of the Lord is a spiritual power that he cannot comprehend. Remember the story about Paul and Silas in the jail, singing songs in the night? How can men sing and be happy in chains? The joy of the Lord is a mysterious thing, but it is part of the fruit of the Spirit, and it breaks the bondage of hurt, anger, and frustration in the mind.

You see, you have to let go of the problem and give it to God in order to have good cheer during tribulation—it's deeper than a mindset. It's a spiritual law for believers because we know that our foundation is Christ Jesus, Who overcame so that we could overcome. He is our substitute, and so whatever problems come, they are not just *our* problems—they are *His* problems, and He told us He already overcame them. This is the foundation of our joy. Jesus is the reason we can laugh or even shout and sing in the middle of a bad situation.

Like all things you use faith for, you break the problem in your mind first by focusing on the spirit and speaking the Word. As you break the problem in your mind with faith and the Word, you begin the energy exchange in the spirit to change the problem. Again, we work from the spirit to the natural—and so when we use the joy of the Lord, which is a fruit of His Spirit, we aren't just sitting around laughing; we are using a spiritual weapon!

I am of good cheer on *purpose*. I go to God in prayer for the release of any frustration, and I hand it over to Him on purpose. I remind myself of the truth on purpose. I discipline myself to do it because I know that it's the only thing that will help me in the heat of tribulation. No matter what the fact of the matter is that I'm looking at in the natural, the truth trumps the facts. So, I use cheer as a weapon because that is exactly what it is.

Do you remember that old cliché, "Kill them with kindness"? Well, when you refuse to doubt that you'll overcome and decide to *"be of good cheer"* in the middle of trouble, you are "killing it with joy"—and your joy *isn't* based on being happy that you've got some troubles. No, your joy is based on Jesus' overcoming of the world when He went to the cross, paid the price, died and rose again, giving you access to His same victory. Your joy comes from *not* doubting that He will not just see you through temporary troubles, but He will also see you through it with joy. What the devil meant for harm, God will turn around for good—and it's all going to be OK in the end, regardless of the messy middle.

Being of good cheer, choosing joy, and laughing in the face of tribulation can't happen unless you KNOW that Jesus (the One Who saved you and filled you with His Spirit) is the ultimate and eternal Winner and Overcomer over all the temporary troubles and tribulations of this world.

You can't be cheerful in times of trouble in a doubtful state of mind—it's just not possible, and you'll just be lying to yourself if you say you can. Faith is a force. Faith is not about lying to yourself about reality; it's choosing to believe Someone is bigger and able to help you change the current reality. We overcome by the blood of the Lamb and the word of our testimony (Revelation 12:11). So, our words need to be about overcoming no matter what.

I've made up my mind that if Jesus has already overcome all the temporary troubles of the world and He lives in me, then He will work through me and His angels will work around me to help me bust through every temporary obstacle. I'll overcome whatever the current trouble is trying to hinder my success.

Again, we know that Jesus is divine and outside the realm of time as we know it. If He was slain before the foundations of the world, then He took care of my problem before it ever arrived, too. You see, you cannot overcome in the natural unless you realize that Jesus has already overcome in the spiritual—and that *you* live and move and have your being in *Him*. It's not the other way around!

Being of Good Cheer Is an Action, It's Not an Emotionally-Based Choice

The Lord really is first in everything, whether you put Him first or not—but it is in your best interest to put Him first. Thinking from a spiritual perspective and doing the things you know to do in obedience to His Word only helps you. It's the "in Christ" life in a nutshell, and the awareness of that will affect every part of your life if you let it.

Anything you do, you're either doing "in your own strength" or "in Christ." Now, which one of those do you think is going to be more joyful, peaceful, and successful in overcoming a situation? Whatever you are doing or going through, you can choose how you're going to do it or go through it. It is easier said than done, because we are human and we love complaining. Our brain itself seems to run on pointing out the negatives. God's Word and His Spirit do the opposite.

You may need to pray and let your emotions out to God to expel them some if they are weighing you down. You will definitely need to "hear" God's Word to build your faith in those times when you want to be of good cheer but can't seem to do it.

I've decided being of good cheer is an action. It's not an emotionally-based choice. You will not feel like being joyful, but you can still choose joy by deciding not to doubt God. The more you make that choice, it's amazing how much more joyful your emotions get. It's about choosing what you know spiritually instead of relying solely on your natural thoughts about things.

Jesus Challenged Us to Believe— He Never Encouraged Us to Doubt

I've had many opportunities to fail—I just decided I wasn't going to take any. I decided that I wasn't going to look at challenges as if I didn't serve a God Who could help me overcome them, learn from them, and grow as a person of faith.

I've had many opportunities to die—and I just decided I wasn't going to take any of those either. I've been shot at three times. I've been almost knifed three times. I've had two separate incidents where some fool tried to electrocute me on stage with the microphones. I've been down in three commercial airplanes too, and guess what? Now I've got my own plane. Some people don't like that, but I don't care. They didn't give it to me, so why should I care that some are mad that I have it?

God has been good and gracious to me, and I make *no* excuses for the blessings of God—just like I make no excuses for getting what I *believe for* in life. I don't follow the religious or secular status quo. "They" aren't my master, and I'm not their slave. I know that God's Word says I can have anything I have the faith to believe for, so why should I allow religion or the secular world's ideas about what I can do or have influence me more than what God said?

Jesus taught us to ask *anything* in His name and to have faith that God would bring it to pass. Jesus taught that faith itself brought on healing and wholeness. Jesus challenged people to simply believe, and He didn't complicate it by saying, "Well, what I *meant* to say was just *try* . . . maybe God will, maybe He won't."

Jesus did not mince words when it came to believing. He consistently preached that we should be living by faith and not doubt God. I firmly believe that it's *doubt* that brings the complications to our mind and to our ability to receive from God—whether it's spiritually, physically, financially, or in any other area. I believe fear is often at the root of doubt, and yet the Word tells us to fear *not* and only *believe* (Luke 8:50).

The Audacity to Believe Is Good for the Soul

I believe with all my heart that God loves it when we just have the audacity to believe His Word and believe for big things. He has no problem with big things; He has no problem with little things either. And I think God just loves it when we live our lives with real honest-to-goodness belief that He loves us and is on our side.

We can have what the Word says we can have and do what He puts on our heart. Challenges are a fact of life, and they come to everyone, but why not see them as opportunities to believe? What's the alternative? Should we just live always complaining, sad and disgusted, or constantly waging an internal battle of why this and why that? NO.

It's pointless to fight the fact that challenges come in life. It's what you are going to *do* in the moment that matters—will you have faith in God or will you have faith in something else? Will you run and give up? Or will you stand up and have joy in the messy middle anyway? These are the kinds of questions that matter because with God, you can handle anything—you do not have to let the circumstances run your mind into the ditch. You can choose faith and choose joy.

I'm just like you. I've got a human mind that sometimes shouts, "You can't!" or "You never will!" But it's in that *moment* that I let the *faith* of God within me rise up. That's the moment I lean on my faith instead, and I do it on purpose. I choose to see the situation from God's "all things are possible" perspective. I bring my problems to Him and let go. I let Him guide me as to what to do, when to do it, and how to do it—and when I stick with what He says, it always turns out in my favor in the end.

So, I don't fight others or myself. I just push the light of God within me up and out to others. I say, "If God said I can, then I can. If God said I'd overcome in His Word, then I will! It doesn't matter what they say, it only matters what You say, God, and what I believe." Faith is a choice I make in the moment. It's a choice I continually reinforce in my own mind. It's a choice I hope you make, too. It's amazing how much easier that choice is to make when you put the Word first—and how much more joyful life is every day that you do.

Doubt Relies on the Senses

IT'S UNSTABLE, TEMPERAMENTAL, AND WON'T LET YOU LOOK AT THE BRIGHT SIDE

I think that one of the hardest things to do is to "unlearn" a bad habit. Once you start a habit, it's hard to quit or break that habit. I see a lot of people who want Jesus as Savior but do not want Him as Lord. They want a rescuer when they fall down, but they don't want to stop doing the things that make them fall.

The moment doubt left Thomas, he easily could say, "My Lord," because if you are a follower of Christ, you know in your spirit that He is the Way, the Truth, and the Life. You know, so when doubt leaves you, it's easy to follow Jesus. Again, doubt is like a blindfold that keeps you from seeing the truth. It's like a pair of shackles that keep you from walking free. It's like two plugs for your ears that cause you to fixate only on the senses and hinder you from hearing the spiritual truth.

What Thomas said to the disciples in private was not just between him and the other disciples. Jesus heard every word and used the situation to teach us the importance of faith. There is no place too far that the Lord's ears can't reach. He hears what we say in our hearts just as clearly as He hears what we say with our mouth.

When Jesus said, *"Thomas, because thou hast seen Me, thou hast believed: blessed are they that have not seen, and yet have believed"* in John 20:29, Jesus was talking about how the blessing is connected to believing.

Doubt Only Relies on the Five Senses

Thomas showed us that it actually takes a lot more effort to doubt. He said there was a lot more action he'd have to do to convince himself that Jesus was alive. He'd have to *see* His hands. He'd have to put his finger in the holes. He'd have to thrust his hand into His side. That's three things—and all of them sensory.

No other disciple had to go through so much just to believe. It was doubt that gave Thomas so much to do! And he was very adamant about doing all that—when, really, all he had to do was just believe. Jesus had told him it would happen when He was teaching them. Mary had said it'd happened. The other disciples had said it, too. All Thomas had to do was listen and be open to the truth.

It's when we start leaning only on our five senses that we start making the believer's life more difficult than it needs to be. Blessed (which means empowered to prosper) is the man who believes without seeing, before he sees, or even if he never sees—our blessing is connected to our believing.

Again, I like to put myself in scriptures and say, "Blessed is Jesse! He has not seen, and yet he believes!" Put your name in there and say that to yourself. Remind yourself that you are a person of faith; not a person of doubt. Don't let thoughts like, "Who do you think you are calling yourself blessed?!" stay if they come in.

You are everything to the Lord. He gave His life for you—and not just to rescue you when you fall, but also to lift you to a blessed place. Life is better when you're blessed! It's better when you simply believe. It's better when you side with hope and faith. There is optimism in believing.

Death wasn't the end for Jesus, and He told all of them that truth. Doubting that truth is what brought them misery. You see, we were created to be a hopeful people, a believing people, and we must sometimes fight for our hope and belief. When doubt entered this world in the Garden, hardship entered. Doubt breeds misery.

God Didn't Say, "Boy, It's Dark Out Here ... Look How Dark It Is!"

As believers, we've been redeemed from the curse of the enemy—but we must choose, each time we have the opportunity to doubt, to reaffirm our choice to believe. It's not enough to just think well; it's important that you speak well. Think and speak in faith. That is the good habit we've got to cultivate. And it's better than unlearning the bad habit of constantly doubting God and just "telling it like it is"—you were made to think higher and further than that.

We serve a God that formed the world and created everything we see with the words of His mouth. His Words have creative power—and they are good words that will lift you up and not tear you down. The Bible tells us that in the beginning, God created the heavens and earth, and the earth was without form and void. Darkness was upon the face of the deep, and the Spirit of the Lord God moved upon the water—and what did God say? God said, "Light be!" I want you to notice that He didn't say, "Boy, it's dark out here . . . look how dark it is out here! I wish it wasn't so dark. I hate darkness. What am I going to do with all this darkness? Sure is dark out here!"

God just said what He wanted. He spoke light into existence—He didn't complain about the current situation but changed it with the words of His mouth. Light would have never existed if God just stared at the darkness and got sad about it. No, He had an intention and a desire to see the light. We have to be that way, too.

Doubt Won't Let You Look at the Bright Side

Doubt is an enemy of light. It hinders hope and keeps you from looking at the bright side. It's a "Yeah, but . . ." kind of killjoy. No matter what God says you can be or have, doubt tries to kill the dream with "Yeah, but . . ." Doubt is full of excuses. Doubt sometimes disguises itself to look like concern or wisdom—but, really, it's just fear playing itself out, trying to protect you from things that it has no power to protect you from. It simply cannot let you look at the bright side because its fixation is always on the dark. It's not the way of God, and so it shouldn't be the way of people living the believing life.

Have you ever seen me sad and depressed? If you've been following my ministry for years, have you ever seen me discouraged, despondent, broke, or miserable? Do I complain all the time on television or social media about how bad things are? No. Am I any better than you or anybody else? No.

I've been attacked in the media ferociously for the blessings of God on my life and ministry. Do you see me crying about it, hiding away over it, or making excuses for the blessing? No.

Deuteronomy 28:6 talks about being blessed coming in and blessed going out. Well, I can say that I am blessed coming in and going out—but I'm also attacked coming in and attacked going out! The blessing of the Lord sometimes comes with its share of persecution. The hundredfold blessing comes with persecution. In Mark 10:30, Jesus made that perfectly plain. And, like I said earlier, He also said that we will have tribulation and trouble in this world, but He told us to be of good cheer anyway because He has overcome this world—and because of that, we can overcome anything that comes our way if we stand in His strength. This is a bright-side way of thinking that is based on the blood of Jesus. It's not a suggestion; it's a command from Jesus Christ.

I Don't Have Optimism—I Have Faith in Jesus

So, just like I don't doubt that Jesus has overcome the world, I don't doubt my own ability to be of good cheer when things aren't going great—He wouldn't have commanded me to be of good cheer if I wasn't capable of doing it. I remind myself of His Word, of His love, and that no weapon formed against me will prosper (Isaiah 54:17). It may be formed against me, sure, but it will not prosper—in other words, it won't ruin my ministry or my life. I know that Jesus overcame, and I will too. That's *not* light optimism. It's simple faith in Jesus. If He said it, it's true.

I know that when I'm under attack, I can either go my way or His way. I can say, "Light be!" so to speak, or I can say, "Boy, it's dark in here!" I choose God's best because I know it's best. I tell my flesh that it can't have its way and that there is no reason to get down when God will save and lift me up—and I have a hand in that lifting. I can have faith in Him. So, I do! Why? Because I know His way is the best way for me. It's the best for my life in general, but it's also the best for my mental well-being.

Some people think that it's the challenges of life that make them strong—but I think it's the joy of the Lord during the challenges that make me strong. The joy of the Lord is my strength. The problems aren't my strength. I don't get stronger just when everything is easy either. I get stronger when I exercise my inner joy *regardless* of external situations. God's Word lifts me up when the world wants to tear me down. His joy gives me cheer when the world wants to see me in anguish. I decided that the world doesn't have the power to steal my joy—I do not give them that right. Why? Because I never learned to doubt God.

If He said His joy is my strength, then I'm going to live a strong life regardless of what "they" say—so let them say what they will! They are going to do it anyway. I just choose to believe what God said over what they say, and guess what? That's how I access my joy. Faith allows you to access joy and any other fruit of the Spirit. Doubt robs you of your ability to access what you need from God in the heat of life's battles—and a lot times, when people attack you, you need strength and joy to get through it. I like to say that "I'm killing it with joy."

Doubt Is Unstable—If You Let It Rule Your Head, You'll Be the Same Way

Doubting God and His Word, and even doubting yourself, robs you of peace and joy in your soul. You may be attacked by others, too. If you are, don't sweat it. No matter what "they" say, they can't take what's in your soul unless you let them. Don't let them. Don't help them by cutting yourself down further, too. Don't join the condemnation party! Be on your own side—and you get on your own side by getting on God's side. Let what *He says* about you be louder in your head than what *they say* about you. That's how you'll be able to look on the bright side of things.

Doubt is unstable. If you let it rule your head, you'll be the same way. But the Word of God will make you stable and help you be consistent. So, get yourself a list of scriptures to speak over yourself daily. Tell your mind Who you belong to and what you're made of. For instance, put yourself in those verses and say things like, "I'm created in God's image. I resemble my Father, God! I'm blessed! He's put His hand of blessing on me—I am fruitful in everything I do, I multiply what I've been given, I replenish the earth, and I subdue whatever rises up against me because I have dominion! I'm loved, and I'm known by God. I have joy and peace, and nothing can rob me of it. I do not fear because the Lord has redeemed me and called me by name. He said, 'You are mine!' and I agree."

If you're unlearning doubt, you might hear your mind say horrible things in response like, "Who do you think you are? Stop bragging! You think you're all that? You think you can do anything like that? You aren't anything and you can't do anything! Stop talking nonsense!" If that happens, remember that doubt is an intruder and an enemy of hope and joy. Do you want to be miserable or joyful? You choose based on whether you believe what God says or believe what the enemy says.

You see, doubt is in opposition to faith—it cannot do anything but condemn you for wanting more or being more. Doubt will try to drag you down. It will accuse you of all sorts of things without merit. It will try to remind you of any mistake you ever made. Think of it like that serpent in the Garden—and do not give it an opportunity to keep running its stinking cruel mouth.

Don't listen to the subtlety of doubt, because if you do, it will just turn into an outright lie. Get your scriptures and speak them regardless of how doubt tries to get your attention. Drown out the noise with something that's going to bring you life and that more abundantly. Just do like me and decide that you will not give doubt a place in your heart. You will not let lies infect your state of being. Joy is your strength, I'm telling you!

Doubt Is Temperamental—
Christians Who Make It a Habit Are Often the Same

Trouble with the outside world understanding a life of faith is understandable to me. The natural man doesn't understand the things of God; they are foolishness to him (1 Corinthians 2:14). So I get why unbelievers attack faith. What I don't get is why believers attack *other* believers on the basis of *believing*! That's a little bit tongue twisting, but you get my point. Nobody attacks faith and blessing in a Christian's life like *other* Christians.

How is so much attacking possible when we are supposed to be one body—you'd swear the arms are trying to tear off the legs, and the teeth are trying to bite off the fingers! The body of Christ has trouble keeping it together!

Why *do* we have church trouble? Why do people get mad at each other in *church*? I'll tell you why—because doubt is temperamental. Some believers enjoy doubting other believers. Some believers enjoy finding what separates them more than what unites them—because they enjoy judgment.

Living in strife with others has become such a habit that they are blindfolded to their own hypocrisy. Philippians 2:3 says that nothing should be done through strife. Many believers have read that scripture, but they doubt it! They must not think it's that bad because they do it so much.

"I don't like the way she said that!" one believer might say, "Look at her problems. It serves her right; always walking around and talking about how she's blessed!" We are called to walk in love with one another. John 13:35 tells us that it is by our love for one another that others will know we've been born of God. Believers know those scriptures and yet do not walk in love with people who sit right around them in church. Why? Temperamental!

Doubting the Word makes you temperamental. It hinders you from looking on the bright side, giving people the benefit of the doubt, and walking in love regardless of whether you agree with people's views or not.

10

Doubt Makes No Attempt to Walk in Love

THE ROOTS OF A LACK-OF-LOVE MENTALITY ARE MANY, BUT GOD CAN HANDLE THEM ALL

Have you ever been around a child that beat their spoon on a dish over and over and over again? Can you picture somebody banging a cymbal completely out of sync with an orchestra trying to play a beautiful piece? That's what the Bible uses as imagery in 1 Corinthians 13:1 to compare us to when we don't walk in love with others. We become irritants to the music God wants the world to hear—the song of love that He is singing to those in need of Him. When we don't walk in love, we become like clanging cymbals that nobody wants to hear . . . except other people who are irritating clanging symbols! It would be funny if it weren't so miserable!

One sure way to know that you doubt God's Word is true is if you make no attempt to follow it. Indifference to act on what you know shows you don't think it's that important, which means you don't think God is very important. That may sound harsh, but it is true. So, you have to ask yourself, "Is walking in love important to me?" And if you can honestly see by your own habits that it's not, then you need to ask God to help you fish out what's keeping you from being a disciple who knows the importance of love. God can and will reveal the reasons in your heart to you if you reach out to Him and seek His help.

The roots of why there is a lack of love aren't too deep or tangled for God. Usually, they are right below the surface if you're brave enough to scratch it! Look, God can reveal that issue and help you to release anything. Whether it's childhood habits learned from others, anger or resentment that has built up over years, or simply pride and the desire to be superior to others—whatever it is at the root—you can release what God reveals to you. So, if it's a struggle, scratch!

This world is not easy, but people learn how to survive, and they sometimes bring that survival of the fittest mentality into the Church. They forget that we're bound by love, and that our faith as believers literally works by love. I always tell people, "Faith is like a car, and it will take you places you never dreamed. But love is like the oil in a car. So, if your faith isn't working, check your love walk. You might be two quarts low!" It takes both to see true godly success, and most of all, to live at peace.

You Would NOT Have Liked the Old Jesse— I Was Lacking in Love and Full of Anger

Take me, for instance. I was an angry man before I got saved, but the love of God that forgave me helped me to forgive others—I had to actively work on letting them go in the beginning, but that was just building a new habit. You don't get great at something by just doing it once, but it becomes second nature to you the more and more you practice. I have had to practice walking in love. I have had to practice being patient. I'm not perfect, but if you knew me as a younger man, you'd think I was a walking miracle because that's how different I am today. It's night and day. When people tell me that I'm so joyful, I know that it's all God—because, buddy, they would NOT like the old Jesse. Thank God, he's dead! Old things have passed away and all things have become new, and, for me, that meant love came and, man, was it new?! It was new!

So, if you're like I was and love for others is lacking, know that you aren't a bad person—you've just got some "new" that needs to get in you! There may be a root you don't realize has taken hold. Maybe, like me, you developed it to survive the hardness of the world from a very young age. Don't worry about that! God can change anything, including you if you bring it to Him and let Him in.

The Roots of a Lack-of-Love Mentality Are Many, but God Can Handle Them All—Go to Him!

For some, anger is rooted in the fear of "not having enough" or being mad at others for "having too much"—that's just lack mentality. Don't worry. God can handle that! You put His Word in your mind daily about it, and He will show that He is a limitless God and that He has an abundant supply, and it's enough for *everyone*. You don't have to shore up in anger. You don't have to scrap with others because they aren't getting what's yours! There's enough for *all* in God.

A lack mentality can spin off into envy and jealousy—but God can handle that, too. A doubt-filled mind can spin off into judgment and criticalness—but God can handle that as well. So, remind yourself that if anything like that rises up, it's just an old habit from your old pre-Jesus self. Remind yourself that you are a new creature in Christ now, and that there is no lack in God, so there is no lack in *you*. Tell yourself that He's El Shaddai, not El Cheapo—His very name means "more than enough!"

Have you ever met someone who felt like it was his or her job to cut everybody rising up down to size? Like they had to keep the playing field level? That's just somebody doubting that God can do His job. It's not any believer's job to cut others down to size, because we don't know what size God made somebody else to be! Nobody died and made us God. He's got His job, and we've got ours—and it's His job to judge, while it's our job to love.

Walking in love isn't always easy, but it is always worth it. It doesn't mean never having an opinion that clashes with another. It doesn't mean you don't get angry. It just means you don't sin against God and yourself by falling into the trap of the enemy—it means you choose to value God's Words over other people's actions. The truth is, we can be a lot harder on others when we aren't aware of the mercy of God at work in our own lives!

It's What Is Coming Out of Your *Heart* That Matters Most— People Pick Up More than You Know

Nobody's perfect. People make mistakes. Love doesn't look the other way and say nothing matters. It also doesn't kick a person when they are down and act holier-than-thou. Love cares too much to do either of those things. Love lets small things go. Love confronts when needed but does it with true concern, for the purpose of helping and not fighting. Love doesn't point out others flaws just to feel better about itself. Love decides that honoring God's Word is more important than fighting to always be right.

How you talk to others matters, but it's what is coming out of your *heart* that matters the most—because people can pick up on that. Some people don't overtly cut others down, but the way they say something reveals that they hate everything! Have you ever met someone like that?

Let's be honest, there are people who are flat "thorns in the flesh" in the church, and then . . . there are people who are complete bushes! You *will* encounter them. You may be one of them! If you are, you probably sometimes think, *God, help me get rid of these thorns!* If so, God will help you, but you will have to practice going to the Pruner. God will help you, and then you just keep on going back to Him until you're not even prickly!

I used to have Tabasco sauce running in my veins, I was so hot-blooded, but God gave me a transfusion of the blood of Christ—and little by little, the more I let Him grow me with His Word, the more the Tabasco left. Now, I'm just flavorful! And now and then, I have to go to God to help me again, but that's alright. We are all works in progress, but let me assure you that God can help you. If you're hot-blooded, He can cool you down. If you're cold, He can warm you up. Don't doubt that. If you doubt it, you'll never change. Have faith in God! The more of His Word you put *in*, the more that will change you, and that change will come *out* in your dealings with people.

Have You Ever Met a Christian That Made You Feel "Scratchy"?

Now, sometimes, as you grow in God, you get very sensitive about what's going on inside of others. Small little personality quirks don't rub you the wrong way much, but you start sensing deeper issues with people—and those things that are hidden in others start creating what I call a "scratchy" feeling in your spirit. Have you ever been around a Christian that rubbed you the wrong way like this and you couldn't figure out why? Every time you got around them you just recoiled, but you just didn't know why? They may even have acted very kindly outwardly, but there was just something in your spirit that you couldn't put your finger on.

When I was a younger Christian, I learned to be very truthful with people when I was picking up something in my spirit about them that rubbed me the wrong way. Sometimes after a service or before it, when I had been flowing in God's Spirit and praying for people, it was like I was fine-tuned to discerning problems with people at a soul level. I was often picking up things that I couldn't identify in others but that I *knew* were wrong.

Back then, I was young and so blunt about it, I wish I'd had more tact. Sometimes I'd just ask them point-blank-blunt things like, "Why am I feeling this scratchy feeling in my spirit when I get around you?"

I'll never forget this situation years ago where I had this preacher who was giving me that feeling every single time I saw him. Outwardly, there was no reason I should feel that way. The man was nice to me. But I felt it strongly, and so one day I just walked up to this preacher, knowing I had to say something—because I couldn't figure out why I just didn't like the man and why I kept wanting to recoil around him.

He saw me walking up to him, and before I could say something, he smiled and said, "How are you doing, Brother Jesse?" I looked at him and said, "I need to ask you a question." He looked at me as if to say "Go ahead," and so, like a kid, I just blurted out, "How come I don't like you?" He looked shocked. But I didn't stop, because it was really bothering me and, really, that question was the bottom line for me. I said, "Because, you see, I love everybody. I like people. I am a people-person, but there is something about you . . . I just don't like. And I don't know what it is, so I am asking you. Now, if I am wrong, you tell me. But why don't I like you? Why do I get scratchy when I get around you?"

Now, even with blunt words like that, this man could tell I was asking him in love—because my attitude, my tone of voice, and my whole vibe was just not in attack mode, and yet I was saying things that people rarely have the guts to say unless they want to fight. I knew I wasn't better than him. I just wanted an answer because I *wanted* to like this guy. I didn't want to pretend and still keep feeling that recoil in my heart. I wanted to just like him!

That preacher looked at me and was just as honest with me as I'd been with him. He said, "Because I'm in *great* sin." I got it then! I was picking up his sin in my spirit, but it wasn't revealed to my mind what it was. I didn't need to know. When he said that, I knew what I had to do. I didn't prod him about what the sin was or judge him into hellfire either. I just looked at him and said, "Well then, it's time to repent."

We prayed, and he repented, and that was that. Immediately, I felt that scratchiness in my spirit lift—so I knew that it was actually a God-moment that had led me to say something. He was ready to let go. In fact, his soul was filled with conflict over whatever it was he had been doing. Right then, he changed. I felt it in my spirit.

You see, when you get rid of what's weighing you down, you stop living divided. That's what happened to that preacher. He looked good on the outside, but he was a divided man. One prayer and one release to God, and through forgiveness, he was able to become one again—just himself, redeemed, and freed from the sin that was creating turmoil in him at a spiritual level. Guess what? I felt at ease around him. No more scratchy feelings!

It's Easier to Walk in Love When You See Yourself as "New"

Love isn't always passive. Love isn't always direct. Love is whatever is needed at the time, according to God's Word and the Spirit of God leading you. You have to do things like that with the right spirit. Even if your words aren't the best, people can sense more than you think. They feel it when you are genuinely interested. Many can pick up whether your motives and intentions are good, so make sure they are.

Now, today, I'm older and wiser, and I'd like to think that I'm better with my words. But if you are a person who lives believing—who makes believing God your habit and enjoys living in the spirit—you too may pick up on what lies inside of others. The believing life separates you from sin. It makes the reality of it repulsive to you—you can still love the people, but the thing eating them up inside becomes something you know needs to go. It's a cancer in the heart of the person that the love and forgiveness of Jesus can wash away.

Jesus is the cure for sin. Sharing that with others in love is my job as an evangelist. It's your job, too, because the Word said all believers are called to be evangelists and reach people for Christ (Mark 16:15). We can't do that living in doubt. We do that living the believing life. We do it being bold enough to follow the Spirit of God within us.

But what happens when we don't see our *own* self in the light of Jesus' forgiveness? Our self-image is important. It colors the way we do everything. It affects how much of God's Word we will believe, and that's not just important for us but to all we come into contact with each day. There are people today who need to see some joy and experience the love of God through you.

I don't like when I hear believers say things like, "Oh, I'm nothing, I'm just a forgiven sinner." To me, that is the wrong frame of mind entirely. All may have sinned and come short of the glory of God, but once we begin living the believing life—when we are saved and choose to believe Jesus—we step into a new position. We are something. Jesus didn't die for nothing! His death purchased our redemption, and our forgiveness may be free to us but it came at a high price to Christ. So, we've got to believe that we are more than just sinners who've been forgiven!

We are *new* creatures in Christ, and old things have passed away. ALL things have become new inside of us. Go read the Word for yourself in 2 Corinthian 5:17. That word *behold* used in the King James means "Look!" In other words, we are supposed to look at ourselves in a different way, and others should see the difference, too. Living the believing life and not the doubting life means we don't just talk; we act. That means if we read that we've been made in God's image and likeness, then we should believe it . . . not just say we believe it.

I've Never Heard God Talking Bad About Himself

I've never heard of God downplaying Who He is or what He's done, like it's nothing. I've never heard of Jesus putting Himself down.

I've never heard of the Holy Spirit making excuses for Who He is and pretending to be less. We are called to be imitators of God as dear children. Doubt about yourself can kill your dreams from the inside out.

If God calls you His handiwork, if He says He's the One Who created your innermost being and knit you together in your mother's womb—that He carefully and wonderfully made you—then who are you to doubt God's work? You just have to walk by faith and not by sight if you don't like what you see! Don't let doubt come in and rob you of a good self-image. Instead, let faith in what *God* said about you lift you up.

Are your thoughts about yourself in line with His? If not, that's doubt. See it as that. Realize that every time you cut yourself down, you are cutting God down—you're doubting that what He did is good and what He said is true.

Humility isn't putting yourself down; humility is knowing that what God thinks is higher in rank than what you think. It's not only lifting others up and seeing them as wonderful, but it's also seeing yourself as God's wonderful handiwork, too. You *are* God's handiwork—that's the truth, and that makes you valuable and wonderful in His sight. So, if that's how He sees you, you need to see *you* that way, too. If that's how God sees others, you need to see others that way, too. This world would be a lot nicer of a place if we all saw each other and ourselves as God does.

Deuteronomy 28:13 says you are the head and not the tail, above and not beneath—that means God sees you as on top. Refuse to doubt it. I don't care what it looks like, you just say what God says about you and you will eventually not only feel like you are that, but you'll see tangible proof of it in your everyday life. Why? Because faith in the goodness of God's Word about you will lift you up. It will change your perspective, and that shift will cause you to act differently—in the way that you should, with love for yourself and others, and with bold faith in God and in yourself. Get rid of doubt and reinforce your new position in your own mind.

If you are holding onto some past thing that is stopping you from loving yourself, let it go. Ask for forgiveness, and let it go. Don't keep dredging up your past to yourself. Actively just let go. After all, if God forgave it, why are you holding it over your own head? That's doubt too. Don't doubt the power of the blood of Jesus for the remission of sins. Don't doubt that all guilt and shame was put on Jesus when He hung on the cross.

When you hold onto old things and beat yourself up over what God has already forgiven, well . . . it's just more doubt! It's doubting the power of the blood of Jesus. Start seeing it that way because the enemy is subtle, but I assure you that *that* is one big way he attacks God's children. He loves to cast doubt on what Jesus did. Guilt and shame are weapons in his arsenal. Faith is the shield that all those fiery darts bounce off of and hit the floor. Do yourself and others a favor by checking yourself—ask yourself where are you doubting God, and where are you doubting yourself? Be honest with your answers, and then work on releasing those doubts one thought or word at a time as they come up.

If you get an old thought, tell yourself you're a new creature and old things are passed away. Tell yourself those are not your thoughts anymore—because you are following the Word, and so you've got Philippians 4:8 thoughts now. Say, "Oh no, that's not my thought! My thoughts are true, noble, just, pure, and lovely—whatever is a good report, and if there's any virtue and anything to praise, that's what I'm thinking about."

If God didn't call you something, you shouldn't call yourself that either. If God wanted you fixating on the old things, He wouldn't have made you a new creature in Christ. If He didn't want you to have a good self-image and walk in love with yourself, He wouldn't have said so many wonderful things about you in His Holy Word to remind you how wonderful you are to Him. So, don't doubt Him!

The Blinding Intensity of Faith

DON'T BE BLINDED BY THE IDEA OF "IT'S TOO GOOD TO BE TRUE"

S ometimes people start out trying to believe, but then they give up. They're blinded by the idea that what God says is "too good to be true." I call that the intensity of faith, and it's blinding to some. I always say that if the light of faith is too bright for you, it's only because your eyes are accustomed to this world . . . and this place has very little faith and way too much darkness.

Remember that just because you haven't experienced something in the past doesn't mean you can't experience it in the future—your past is not how you measure the things of God! His ways and His thoughts are higher than natural ways and thoughts (Isaiah 55:8-9). Faith is intense because it takes you out of your natural comfort zone and moves your perspective higher, and so if you want what God says, then you have to move higher.

You have to be willing to look into the light of His love for you, because the faith you will gain by hearing the Word works by love. You must believe that God loves you. If not, how can you have faith in what He says? What He says is said from a place of love, and that is a very intense and pure place. It's a divine love, and maybe one that you've never experienced in your past. Everything God has is bright and pure.

There is light in every promise from God. They are all "too good to be true" if you are only looking at the natural ways of this world—

but God's ways aren't man's ways. If a person tells you something, you cannot bank on it being true. You know that human nature is flawed and that people lie. Again, God is not a man that He should lie.

When Guilt and Shame Are Linked to Doubting God

Divine truth is bright. The Gospel is so pure that it makes those who love darkness recoil and gnash their teeth in hatred. As believers, we are drawn to the light because we know that it's full of love—and anything God says to us is for our own benefit, even if it corrects us. So, whenever we begin to have faith in Him, we are choosing to look headlong into the purity of His light and love. God is not passive. He is pure. God doesn't look the other way when it comes to our sin. He uses the blood of Jesus to wash it away from us. That's not a passive and loving Father. That's a just and loving Father. God is strong, and yet He is long-suffering with us. His mercy and grace aren't cheap; they came at the price of His only Son.

This is why the love of Christ is so overwhelming at times to those of us who've accepted Christ. Just thinking about what Jesus did for us, by taking our sins upon Himself on the cross, is an overwhelming thought—because it's "too good to be true" in the natural that any man would do this for others, even others that bitterly hate him.

Jesus presented us with a Gospel so pure that it is blinding for some. Even if they accept salvation, they will often wade through life in guilt over their past—the same past that the blood of Jesus washed away. He doesn't want the light of His glorious Gospel blinding us to the details of our redemption. He wants us to see ourselves in the light of His Son and realize that the great sacrifice for our sins also includes our guilt and shame.

For many people, doubting God is linked to guilt and shame. They doubt God will do what He said for them because they believe they are unworthy—that the mistakes they made are still hanging onto them. The intensity of faith is too much for them, and they are blinded by the light of His forgiveness.

Unworthiness, once you accept Christ's sacrifice for your sins, is a form of doubt. It's saying you don't think the blood of Jesus is good enough to wash your sins away. From that state of mind, it's easy to see why even good believers say, "it's too good to be true" when they are taught about other things in the Word like healing or abundance in life.

If the baseline of your salvation is the remission of sins and a person can't accept that even *that* is taken care of, then it's going to be very hard to move on to anything else. This type of person may say that they want to be healed or blessed, but inside they doubt that God will heal or bless them. They believe *others* may receive but doubt that *they* can receive.

Listen to me. If you believe God is good and that His Word is true for somebody else, you should believe the same for yourself—because the same Jesus died and rose again for us all. Your sin can't be bad enough to overcome the blood. Somebody else's sin may be miniscule to your old sin, but guess what? It's all sin. It's all washed under the blood. And it's time for us to see ourselves for who we are—not sinners saved by grace but new creatures in Christ, where old things have passed away and all things have become new. That's how you get rid of that "unworthy" junk that is just a form of doubt. Take those shackles off. Jesus died so that you could walk free.

When Being Shackled with Debt Is Linked to Doubt

Many people tell me that they are shackled in debt, but I've come to see that one key component to getting out of debt and staying out is to renew the mind concerning finances—to get rid of the doubt that tells you that "you have to live this way." To be free, you have to see yourself as free. Many people can't imagine living without debt, and that's a problem. It's one very real reason that they keep perpetuating the same debt-filled ways of life.

I tell people that in order to get out of debt, they have to start seeing themselves as people who *can* be debt free—they have to start thinking of themselves as lenders instead of borrowers, as the scripture says we can be (Deuteronomy 28:12). They have to start seeing themselves as able, through God's blessing, to be the kind of person who owes no man anything but to love him, as Romans 13:8 says. Faith in God's power and in our own power comes the same way—by hearing, and hearing the Word of God (Romans 10:17).

We can't keep thinking, believing, and saying the same things and expect to magically start doing different things. That's why so many people start off good but give up. They have good actions at the start, but they never dealt with the mindset that got them in trouble in the first place.

People tend to follow patterns and will go back to what is most common in their own heart and mind. I've seen people do all the right things in the natural, like being aware of bad habits, getting a plan in place, and starting to pay things off, but end up in just as much debt down the road. Their debt-free lifestyle didn't last. Why? They didn't deal with the root problem. So, they came back to living the way that was most familiar.

You see, if you don't renew your mind and let go of doubt in your heart about debt or anything else really, you'll end up in the same place you started later in life. This is why it's so important to focus on your thoughts, even in something as practical as working to become debt free. This is why you need to get to a place where you don't doubt God's ability to bless you and give you concepts and insights that will help you. This is also why you need to get to a place in your mind that you don't doubt your ability to live life the way He said you could—free from debt.

Remember, a lot of people are debt free but broke. There are tons of debt free people living on the streets! Just because you don't have debt doesn't mean you have anything at all. The point is not only to be free from the debt that shackles you, but also to live in faith that Jehovah-Jirah (the name for God as our Provider) is always with you providing what you need and desire as you focus your faith. Spiritually, physically, and even financially, we need to see ourselves as houses of God that contain His Spirit—and His Spirit is not one Who is bound by fear and lack.

Sometimes, a person who has accepted the lies of a lack mindset will be compelled to waste money as a way to fill an emotional need. They buy things they don't even *want* just to have the thrill of buying something new, when they already have a ton of debt that needs to be dealt with! God's Word calls us to be wise stewards of what we have just as it tells us to believe Him for all the desires of our heart. He's never trying to limit our blessings, but He does want us to root out the areas where we're lacking inside. Only He can fill those spaces, and when He comes in, we easily get rid of habits that cause us to lose out in the end.

God can help you with whatever inner problem that brings outer problems, but you must help yourself, too—and step one is building faith that you have everything you need in Christ spiritually. Let that shift your emotions. Everything else that you need or desire is in addition to that spiritually "full" state of being. Let all your desires rise up without fear, knowing that God will give us freely all things to enjoy in life, but we must see Him as the Source—and have faith in His ability to guide us in even the smallest practical things in this life, including finances. All the "things" are added to you after you put Him first. Seeking first the kingdom is not about Heaven; it's about seeking first His way of doing things in life (Matthew 6:33).

So, while this world sells us a lie that we have to live in debt, that there is no other way to get ahead, we can stop listening to the lie. We can come to a place where we are so filled with what God said that what the world says doesn't fit. Again, remember that faith in God and in yourself to become debt free is going to come just like any other faith—by hearing, and hearing the Word.

If You Keep Saying What You Don't Want, You'll Keep Getting What You Don't Want

Watch your lips. You can read all the Word you want, but if you keep saying what you don't want, you'll keep getting what you don't want. If you tell yourself you "can't" when God said you "can," you are doubting God's ability just as much as you're doubting your own—and why would you want to do that if you want to be blessed? There are enough people in this world to drag you down; don't add to it.

Remember that it's hard to get something you don't believe you can have. So, work on believing you can have what God said.

If that's your issue, focus on verses that deal with blessings—and not just needs, but desires. God can go over and above just needs, and Jesus told us to ask for what we desire in His name. A lot of people don't believe that, and that's why they don't get it! They learned to doubt Jesus Himself, and they get the fruit of their own lips.

You must sow seeds toward your future, and every word you say is a seed. So, plant the Word; don't just repeat it and leave it. Take a hold of it in your heart. Make it personal because faith *must* be personal to work, whether it's about spiritual, physical, or financial things. You can't make much headway on secondhand faith, but you can go all the way with your own faith. The Word that calls you blessed in the city, blessed in the field, blessed coming in, and blessed going out matters—the more you really believe yourself to be blessed, the more blessings will come.

Clean out the old ways of thinking. Replace them with God's Word, which is His way of thinking. Get rid of doubt and you'll get rid of the root of debt. Remember, what God says about you is final—not what this world says. This is some of what God says: The blessing of the Lord is on you and it brings wealth with no sorrow (Proverbs 10:22). God has given you the ability to produce wealth and establish His covenant on this earth (Deuteronomy 8:18). God's favor surrounds you like a shield (Psalm 5:12). God says that if you respect Him, you will lack nothing (Psalm 34:9).

Read Deuteronomy 28:2-8. Think of it like it's God talking directly to you, because you are the seed of Abraham through Christ Jesus' work, so you are one of God's chosen. Read about how the blessing will come upon you, even overtake you, when you obey the Lord. Read how you'll be blessed everywhere you go, and how even your possessions will be blessed. Yes, the devil will fight it, but so what! The enemy can come at you one way, but he will flee seven ways. God will command the blessing to come upon you—and you'll be blessed in your storehouse (this is in whatever area you store wealth, which, in modern times, would usually be a bank). Realize that according to the Word, God will bless every single thing you set your hand to do.

Now, that's just a little bit of scripture—but start with a little, knowing that even just one Word from God is enough to make radical changes to your mindset. Read the last two paragraphs again and realize that if you start believing that about yourself, you are going to start thinking, talking, and acting differently! You'll end up like 3 John 2. You'll end up using the Word to prosper at a soul level first (mind/will/emotions)—and out of a prosperous soul, you will begin to prosper in ALL things and live in health, too. That's what 3 John 2 says, and guess what? I believe it! In fact, I never learned to doubt it!

So, if someone who's mind is stuck in the world's system starts criticizing me, that's why I say things like, "Don't get mad at me if wealth and riches are in my house! I didn't say it, God did. I just repeated it, believed it, and received it." They aren't criticizing just me, they are criticizing God because He's the One Who said it—I just believed He would do it. I believed and didn't doubt, and He brought it to pass. So, let people criticize if they want. What do I care? I'd rather be on God's side than the world's side anyway!

Life and Death Are in the Power of the Tongue—The Anointing for Healing Flows Best with Others

There's a reason James 5:14-15 encourages the sick to go to the elders of the church and have hands laid on them—it's because our combined faith is greater than our singular faith. Unity is powerful, and the anointing of God is stronger when we come together with others of like precious faith.

My wife is the pastor of the church at our ministry headquarters. I travel most of the time, but I make a point to be in the church as often as I can. I consider the congregation my spiritual family, and I love being with them. In my church, I've seen many who've gone through some pretty tough battles. A man named Darryl is one of them—the doctors had told him he didn't have long to live, and I remember being in that hospital room as he fought to breathe. Yet, in the midst of that struggle, Darryl had faith in God. Those around him were believing in faith for his recovery, too. None of us can know the heart of another person, but when someone is struggling and saying they are believing God, I believe that if we care about them, we should set our faith in line with what they want. Not everyone wants to fight. Some get weary and give up. But for those who are believing God, well, I'm going to believe God with them—I'm not going to deny the problem, but I'm going to deny its right to touch one of God's beloved.

Looking at Darryl, I realized that he may have thought he needed us, but we needed him, too. We need each other in the faith. The anointing flows best when we are in unity, praying together and being together in a unified state of belief. Well, Darryl may have shocked the doctors when he recovered instead of dying, but we were not shocked—we were just seeing the physical proof of what we'd believed all along . . . that Darryl would be healed.

We believed he'd be healed when he was first diagnosed with a bad report. We believed when he seemed, by all accounts, to get worse. We believed when the doctors told him death was near. In other words, our faith in God didn't change with the circumstances—it just got stronger. I've found that the most blessed state to live in is to believe God without physical proof. Your "evidence" must be in the faith itself. Hebrews 11:1 says it this way, *"Now faith is the substance of things hoped for, the evidence of things not seen."*

To this day, when I see Darryl, I often tell him, "You ain't going anywhere without us!" I want him to know that our faith as a congregation isn't singular—we are in faith together, and that includes the struggles. People have asked me, "Well, what would have happened if he'd died?" They don't typically like my response. "Well, he would go to Heaven," I said, "but he wasn't ready to go. So, leave him alone, and set your faith with his."

I believe that *"Death and life are in the power of the tongue: and they that love it shall eat the fruit thereof"* (Proverbs 18:21). We shouldn't bring doubt into a situation where someone is fighting for his or her life—we shouldn't bring doubt anywhere! If death and life are in the power of the tongue, then we should be people who speak *life.* We should *love life.* Many believers say they love life but speak death all the time.

You're Sowing Word-Seeds Toward Your Future Every Day, So Be Sure to Plant What You Like and Want to Eat

Have you ever heard someone pray a wonderful prayer of faith and then immediately cancel it out with negativity afterwards? If the only words of life you say are during a prayer, that's a problem—because every word is a seed that is being planted. Again, think of this verse: *"Death and life are in the power of the tongue: and they that love it shall eat the fruit thereof."* Ask yourself, "If I only plant a few word-seeds of life but plant acres and acres of death-seeds with my mouth, what do I think I'll eat the most of in my life?"

Death or life, how do we know what we love more? All we have to do is listen to the words coming out of our own mouth. Remember, our words don't just happen—it is out of the abundance of the heart that the mouth speaks (Luke 6:45). So, what we say the most comes from what we believe the most. Every day, we are cultivating our future. Every day, we are sowing. That means we need to plant what we want to eat!

Some people get flat mad when I use this verse when talking about healing—they would rather be nice than truthful, and they get angry thinking about someone who didn't see healing in this lifetime. They want to take it out on me, but I refuse to take the bait. Hebrews 11:35-39 gives us a list of people who died "in faith," and all of them are in Heaven today—so if someone loses a battle, it doesn't mean they lost the war. In this world we have tribulation and trouble, but we overcome when we choose to have faith anyway and be of good cheer, knowing that Jesus has already overcome. In Him, we overcome, too.

On my dying breath, I will believe God—I don't care what others think or say because it's only what God says that will last forever. Heaven and earth will pass away, but His Words will never pass away. So, I choose Hebrews 11:1 knowing I'm in a blessed state when I don't have physical proof yet of what I am believing for in faith—it's how I know I'm on my way to seeing manifestations.

I don't want to be an "I'll believe it when I see it" doubting Thomas kind of man. I don't want to be an Eve kind of believer either, who listens to the devil long enough to be tempted by his lies. No, I've decided that I want to be what Jesus said is best. I want to "believe without seeing" because Jesus called that best. I want to be obedient to whatever God says because I know if God is saying it, then it's in my best interest—spiritually, physically, financially, and in every other way that pertains to this life.

Sometimes We Need to Be Brought to the End of Our Wits

SO THAT WE MAY COME TO THE BEGINNING OF OUR FAITH

Have you ever been at your wits' end? I believe that sometimes we need to be brought to the end of our wits so that we may come to the beginning of our faith. There have been times when I've done everything I know to do and can't think of one more thing to do—this is usually when I've been working in my own strength. It's not faith to work solely in your own strength. There are many things you can do on your own, but why would you want to? Anything worth doing is worthy of doing in faith.

I believe that sometimes we can think we are living by faith just because we talk to God about a problem. Man, I've talked so much to God about a problem that I just knew He was waiting for me to shut up! I'm serious. I wasn't talking to Him with hope; I was just complaining. I believe there are times that we need to just shut our mouths because all we are doing is rehearsing the problem—and there's no peace in that, even if we are rehearsing those problems over and over with God! That's not praying in faith. Peace comes when you pray in faith, but it doesn't come when you pray in complaint! This is what I mean when I say that sometimes we need to be brought to the end our wits so that we may come to the beginning of our faith. It's a critical moment when we realize that what we're doing isn't giving us any peace—and so we have to lay down our "wits" and start talking to God in faith that He is the Answer, and He has the answer to every problem we could ever find ourselves in.

Rehearse the Answer and Not the Problem

Praising God can break the complaint cycle. Praising God in the midst of trouble can break spiritual or emotional bonds that may have us locked in a cycle of thinking only about the problem. Praise lifts our heart higher than we can go by mere intellect alone. We can't always think our way out of a situation, especially if the problem is spiritual or emotional. Praise is one way of lifting up the answer higher than whatever problem may be that is bothering us. It helps us release our problems to God without even mentioning them. It is our faith at work, because when we praise in the midst of trouble, we are reminding ourselves that God is our answer and He is bigger than any problem we could ever have.

You can also rehearse the answer by using the Word of God as a weapon—it's not called the sword of the Spirit for nothing! The Word is living and active, and when we put faith in it and let it come out of our heart and mouth, it breaks the cycle of complaint, too. It opens a pathway for us to rise higher, to let "I've come to my wits' end" go in favor of "I'm ready to start thinking and living by faith." There is a scripture verse for every struggle, but not one can bring us peace if we don't have faith and start saying what God says instead of what we think. Like I said, sometimes we've got to get to our "wits' end" before we realize that we need to switch gears and begin looking at the problem through the lens of faith in God.

Are we relying on Him or not? Do we believe He can help or not? Do we believe that He can cause us to triumph or not? Do we believe that we have the mind of Christ and the ability to tap into His anointing or not? Do we believe that no matter what happens, all things will work out for good for those who love God or not? Will He supply all our needs according to His riches in glory or not? Are we even realizing that "in glory" is not a natural place but a spiritual place—that we pull riches from the spiritual to the natural through the substance of powerful energy we call faith?

So, if we complain all day long about something we should have faith in God over, we have to ask ourselves if our soul is prospering or is our soul in poverty? We are God's beloved, and He wishes above all things that we prosper and be in health—but natural prosperity and health for the believer is inextricably linked to whether our soul (mind/will/emotions) is prospering or not (3 John 2).

I know faith can seem hard, but it's better for you to look at it like it's simple. I didn't say easy! I said simple, and there is a difference. For myself, I've decided that I am not going to muddy myself in the gray areas when my faith in God should be black and white. I don't want to water down my faith with doubt—that's wading in "wits' middle" and it only ends up leading to "wits' end!"

Either it's faith or sin, which is defined as missing the mark. Now, I know that "it's faith or sin" sounds harsh, but that is what God said in Romans 14:23. So, don't get mad at me for believing and repeating God! Faith really is simple. It's not muddy gray. It's pure, even when it feels tough to hear. So, I've decided that I'm either hitting the mark (faith) by trusting God or missing the mark (sin) by doubting God. I decided a long time ago to aim for faith, not sin! It's that simple. Again, I'm not saying it's easy! But it is a very clean and simple way to think and to live, and I've seen over and over again how it leads to triumph over all sorts of problems and "impossible" situations. God is good!

I Brought My Wife to Her Wits' End!

I was an impossible situation. I was one of those people who nobody thought would ever find God, much less talk about God. I was one of those "hopeless cases" as a young man, and I'm pretty sure I brought my wife Cathy to her wits' end many times! When I think back on the beginning of our marriage, I can tell you that the first five years were hell on earth—and it was all because of me.

I was a bad husband. I'm talking bad! I did whatever I wanted, when I wanted, and I didn't care if anybody saw me. She endured a lot, and I was so selfish I didn't even notice or care. Back in those days, fixated on my music career, I drank all the time and did drugs—

and I had groupies who'd come to the door and ask my wife if they could sleep with me.

Now, you wouldn't know it today, but I was pretty good looking when I was young. I know . . . you have to "see it by faith" now, but back then, I had a body that didn't look too bad. I had a six-pack then. Now, I've got a keg! It was the 60s and 70s; they called it the age of Aquarius and free love.

I was working on the same circuit as Led Zeppelin and ZZ Top and those kinds of bands, and Cathy and I traveled and lived in hotel rooms. These women would find out what hotel I was in, knock on the door, and literally ask to go to bed with me. I would be standing behind the door when Cathy answered it, whispering, "C'mon, Cathy! C'mon!" Would you stay married to an idiot like that?

Cathy had come to her wits' end with me, and who could blame her? But she didn't give up on me; she decided to make her wits' end the beginning of faith. Thank God she did, because I don't think I'd be here today if she hadn't. My mother used to have this saying she'd say when she talked about me: "He's getting saved whether he likes it or not! It's just his tough luck he was born to me!" Cathy took that to heart and started saying to herself, "He's getting saved whether he likes it or not. It's just his tough luck he is married to me." Between my wife and my mother, I was being covered with prayer, and although I hated it, it eventually worked.

My mother was always praying for me. God would literally show her where I was when I was in the depths of sin, and she'd call me. I'll never forget my mother calling a bar in Mexico and interrupting my partying to tell me she was praying for me. I'd always ask her how she found me, and she would just say, "I was praying and God showed me . . ." and then she'd describe where I was and start preaching to me. It blew me away.

My wife didn't have that gift, but she locked her faith onto me anyway. It takes greater faith to not see and yet believe, and Cathy had faith. She said she began to see that the problem wasn't me; it was who I was serving. She began to see me as lost and in need of Christ. So, my mother and Cathy made me their project! They put me in what they called "the crosshairs" of faith. Like looking through a gun-scope at their target, they prayed for me with intensity! Why? Because they'd come to their wits' end with me! Sometimes, it's only when we come to our wit's end that strong faith can take over. Faith becomes the weapon it always has been when a believer decides to finally pick it up and take aim.

While my mother may have had supernatural gifts of sight and the prophetic, she was still judgmental and hard, and I wanted to get as far away from that as I could. My wife, on the other hand, began to see everything I did through a different lens—she saw through love and faith, and began saying in her heart that all I needed was Jesus. This affected how she talked to me; even if she was strong, she wasn't unkind. I was unkind! I was the idiot.

Cathy says that she didn't see what I did as "me" once she got saved and started believing God for me to be saved, too. It didn't matter how drunk I got; she stuck to her faith. It didn't matter if I had so much drugs in my system that the skin on my chest was filled with red and purple blotches; she stuck to her faith. She didn't let what I said draw her into a fight, she just stuck to her faith in God that one day I would accept Him as Savior. It worked. It didn't work overnight, but it worked. Her faith gave her strength when many would have given up—but that's what faith does. It brings you peace in the midst of a storm. It shines a light on the real problem and not just on the many side effects of the problem.

Don't let the devil lie to you that your faith doesn't work—it works in ways you may never realize. All people have free will, but when you focus your energy on the power of love and faith and direct it toward someone, you are doing powerful work. You're making spiritual strides in fighting the very things that are holding them back from knowing God in a real way.

Nobody gets judged into the kingdom. Nobody gets scolded into kingdom. They sure don't get cussed and complained at into the kingdom. We are to be *loved* into the kingdom! We are brought in by prayers of faith and love—and not passively, but by fervent faith and love. It got to a point where Cathy would pray over me when I was sleeping. Sometimes I wasn't all the way to sleep yet and I'd feel her fingers come across the sheets. She'd put her hand ever so slightly on my shoulder and whisper, "Come out, devil!" I'd say, "Hey, woman, get your hand off me. I'm awake!" We laugh about it now, but there were many nights she just laid hands on me when I didn't even know it. There were many times she prayed and didn't give up.

I want you to know that walking in love with somebody who acts like the devil and choosing to put them in the crosshairs of your faith is an aggressive combination—and it's not for the faint of heart. It is for those who've come to their wits' end! It's for those who've had enough of trying to do it on their own, and who know that they need God. That's the good fight of faith in action, and it's worth it. I wouldn't be here today if Cathy hadn't fought it and won. As I said, she just had to come to her wits' end so that she could come to the beginning of her faith in what God could do.

Today, Cathy and I work together in the ministry—she's my pastor and my wife! And I'm so blessed to have her in my life all these years. We may have started our marriage with a few years of hell, but there have been decades and decades of heavenly times ever since God came into the picture. He changed me at the core, and I was never the same after I accepted Him into my life. I look at Cathy today and believe that God selected her for me even when I was just a sinner. God knew what kind of person I needed. He knew what He had in store for us, too, if we'd follow Him. I've been married to Cathy since 1970, and we are still going strong today—working together for the cause of Christ and enjoying each other's company . . . almost every day! Ha!

I'm Not Going to Trade in My Passion No Matter My Age— I'd Rather Be Called a Fanatic than Stagnant and Apathetic

I've found that when you live by faith, those who live by mediocrity will consider you a fanatic—but I've decided I don't care about that. I'm never settling for the status quo as a believer when God created me to live with an abundant mindset. I decided a long time ago that I'm not afraid of being called names. God has put His name on me, and that is more important to me than the criticisms of people who'd rather cling to fear.

I've decided I don't need or want to live with mental anemia— I'd rather be called a fanatic than be stagnant in life or apathetic about the truth. If I'm living anyway, I want to *live*. I'm not going to trade in my passion no matter my age. I'm not going to just exist until I go home to be with Jesus—I'm going to believe Him right here and right now, and live with purpose, tenacity, and confidence.

Let me tell you something, if you choose to live that way, you *may* be called a fanatic, but you are *definitely* going to encounter resistance! One area that I've been cut down the most in Christian circles is my belief in Jesus' hundredfold teaching (Mark 4 and Mark 10:30). I believe He will bless my giving and I'll reap multiplied blessings if I faint not. Even though these things are right there in the Bible, Christians hate that I talk about it. Oh, I don't think they care if I believe it for myself, but they do not want me sharing Jesus' teaching on this with others. It is too controversial. It's not the status quo. Many consider it dangerous and even heresy.

Faith is confrontational to many people, and especially Christians. Persecution for the Word's sake is real—and it comes when you choose not to doubt. Unbelievers might call you crazy. Believers may think you're dangerous. Just remember that some believers are so invested in their mindset of fear and insufficiency that they will attack anyone who thinks otherwise.

So, your faith may clash with fearful believers because their beliefs about what God will or will not do are in such contrast to your own. They've got a lifestyle of doubt and are invested in upholding the status quo. Some live in apathy. They've become so indifferent to what Jesus said that they are stagnant. So, when you don't settle, it shines a light on how they are always settling . . . and that's unsettling for them! When you have passion, it shines a light on their numbness. When you speak in faith, it shines a light on all their many doubts. All of that creates tension, but at some point you have to realize that everyone has a free-will-right to believe or not—and if you want the results of faith, you must use faith even if it isn't common in the lives of those you know.

As for me, I don't care if my faith in the hundredfold teaching of Christ is unsettling or irritating to some. I believe and teach it anyway. Why? Because I want all that God's Word said I could have—spiritually, physically, and financially, too. What "they" say can't compete in my mind to what Jesus said, and besides, the Word warns me straight up that the hundredfold comes "with persecution." The Bible makes that plain. So, when they persecute me, I remind myself of that. I look at my harvest and enjoy the fruit of my seeds! Let status-quo-believers water down the Word if they want to. Let them choose what they will believe. I choose to not be stagnant in my giving and in my receiving—I refuse mental anemia and the apathetic mindset that goes along with it. Jesus was controversial in His life on earth, and His Words are still controversial today. I'm willing to take the heat for what I believe.

When I hear the word "fanatic," I don't think of a terrorist—I choose to think of it like the word "fan." I like football. I enjoy watching the Super Bowl every year that I can. When I pick a team to cheer for, I'm choosing to be a fan. Have you ever seen some of those people at the Super Bowl who dance and shout for their team on TV? They are obvious fans of the game. I'm a fan of the New Orleans Saints. I'm not apathetic about whether they win or not—I'm not indifferent! I want them to win, and every year I'm pulling for them to make it to the Super Bowl. Any good football fan isn't afraid to show that they have passion for their team.

Well, I'm passionate for God and the teachings of His Word more than I am for any sports team. I may like the Saints, but I love God—and so I am a passionate fan about whatever God says and God promotes as good. If He said I can have something in His Word, then I don't dismiss it. I'm not living a fatigued, status-quo-life of religious doubt—I refuse to let doubt wear me down mentally. I refuse to let that happen to me, and I hope you refuse to let that happen to you, too! You just flat don't have to live that way no matter what the Church or the world says.

Some People Have Excellent Sight but Poor Perception

DOUBT RAISES QUESTIONS THAT DON'T DESERVE ANSWERS

P erception is a funny thing. My wife tries on clothes and asks me things like, "Does this make me look fat?" THAT is a trick question, and we both know it. Now, my wife was skinny all her life. She could eat a five-gallon ice cream bucket a week and still not gain an ounce. Me? I smell fried chicken and five pounds jumps on me. After about 55 years old, I'd say Cathy started to put on a little weight—she was having hot flashes and all that stuff. I loved it! For yeeeeears, she'd say, "Just suck on some ice cubes, Jesse, when you want some ice cream." Then, she'd eat a bowl of butter pecan the size of a basketball. She had no concept of what it meant to struggle with weight.

So, when she did start putting on a few pounds, I was thrilled. "You see?!" I'd say, "You see now what it's like, don't you? Yeaaaah-hhhh, now you know!" and I'd laugh and laugh. Plus, I liked how she looked with some more meat on her. I especially liked those hot flashes at night because for once in our marriage, she didn't come to bed shivering and covered up like Mother Teresa. I thought, *Thank you, Jesus!* I'd tell her, "Just take it off, Mama, do what you gotta do . . . this is great!"

So, when she'd come from her closet and ask me things like, "Do you think this makes me look fat?" I'd think to myself, *You know it makes you look fat. Why? Because you are getting a little fat!*

And I love it! Just ask me if I think you look good because that answer won't get me into any trouble. I love how you look! I don't know why people are so hard on each other when it comes to weight—I always think, *If you like you, then I like you! Why are you trying to please other people?* The reality is that if you have to ask, then you probably already have great eyesight . . . but a real poor perception of yourself!

Many people have great sight but poor perception. It takes guts to look at a situation, no matter what it is, with two open eyes and an open mind. It's hard for people to be honest with themselves when they don't really want to perceive the truth. Sometimes, as believers, we can see a problem in our life, but we don't perceive it for what it is—we think it's an outward thing when, really, it's an inward thing.

We Must Not Just "See" Ourselves, but We Must Perceive the Heart of the Matter

How can we perceive answers if we aren't willing to really look at the problems in our lives? I believe God and the Word He's given us can help us perceive answers, because His truth always shines a light on the real problem—not just the symptoms of a problem. I believe that's why so many people don't complete their dreams and live regretting it. They simply refused to look at problems in their way for what they really were: obstacles to overcome with faith, tenacity, and heart. Instead, they looked at themselves with so much doubt and fixated on the problem so long that the dream faded away.

Dreams are in our hearts for a reason—and they aren't meant to lie dormant or be pushed down. Sometimes we have to look at our reasons for NOT trying or going for them. We have to be brave enough to access the reasons behind our choice to ignore them. We shouldn't lie to ourselves. We should try to get to the heart of the matter and ask ourselves things like, "What is behind the stall? What is behind the lack of will? What is behind the doubt of oneself or the doubt of others? Why 'can't' it be done? What is the heart issue keeping you from moving forward?" It usually comes down to fear, plain and simple. That's all self-doubt is, FEAR.

When faith is weak and doubt is strong, your judgment will be weakened. Some people have excellent sight but poor perception. They can't decide what is good or not for them. The Holy Spirit can guide us into all truth. That is what Jesus said the Holy Spirit does (John 16:13). If we don't allow the Holy Spirit a place in our lives to guide us in all truth, what will we do? We will just lean on our own understanding and that's *not* good! Our own understanding will always give us the easy "can't" way out. The Word builds our faith for better, though, and the Holy Spirit guides us in all truth so that we can change our thinking about ourselves and make practical decisions from a place of wisdom.

My Daddy's Desire Was So Small, He Thought It Didn't Matter—but It Did

"I'm getting older now and I just can't do that," I've heard people say. And yet we have examples of older people fulfilling lifelong ambitions or dreams all over the world. Growth doesn't stop when you get to a certain age. If you're breathing, you can grow and learn something new—or accomplish what you always wanted to accomplish. Sometimes there are "small" dreams that are extremely important to a person. They're seen as so small that they don't matter—but that's just because the person has great sight but poor perception!

If a good desire is in your heart, then it matters. I remember my Dad saying, "Jesse, I'm having a hard time walking." He was in his 80s then.

I said, "Do you know why, Dad?"

He said, "No."

I said, "Because all you do all day long is SIT!" He laughed.

I said, "Get up, Dad."

"But I can't walk far," he said.

I said, "I'm not asking you to walk a mile, Dad. I'm asking this: How about you get up and walk from your house to the mailbox every day?" A muscle will react to being exercised no matter how old you are—even with just a little effort.

He said, "My arms are so flabby."

"Dad, get a one pound weight," I said, "and while you are sitting here, do this" and I showed him an arm curl.

It wasn't a week and a half later that he called me, "Guess what? I can feel my muscle in my arm!"

I said, "Did you get a dumbbell?"

"No," he said, "No, I got a one pound bag of sugar."

Then, he started making little walks to the mailbox and called me again. "Man," he said, "Jesse, I'm doing it!"

I said, "Dad, muscle will respond but don't overdue it. Nobody's asking you to run a mile or do a marathon. But what I am saying is, just do *something*. That way, if you decide you want to get up by yourself without needing help, you have exercised your body enough that you have the strength to do it."

The mind is a muscle of sorts, too. If you continually say, "I'm getting so old" or "My body is breaking down" or anything like that, you are training the muscle of your mind to believe what you say. It will steal all ambition from you. It'll take away your hope to continually tell yourself what you can't do—so don't do that to yourself.

Moses was a 120 years old and climbing a mountain. Abraham was making babies at 100 years old. Sarah was having a kid at 90 years old. There are big and small dreams in all of us. Who knows what you will do when your perception of what you can do grows? When faith is weak, it suspends and weakens judgment—but when our faith is strong, we realize that "can't" is just a word, and it's most often not even true. You can do all things through Christ that gives you strength, and nothing is impossible for those who believe.

We Were Called to Trust, We Weren't Called to Treat Faith Like Some Mental Exercise

I can't tell you how many times, when Cathy and I were first starting out as believers, that we saved our money so we could give in special offerings at church. When we knew there was a guest speaker coming, we planned for it. We didn't have much, but we trusted that God would always provide for us if we put Him first in our lives.

Back then, when we went out to eat dinner, it wasn't to somewhere fancy—we went to McDonald's because it was cheap. Plus,

I love a good Quarter Pounder with Cheese, and back then, my kid ate more ketchup than fries. She'd dip that fry into the ketchup over and over until it was wet and limp. But we didn't feel like it was some great sacrifice, because we wanted to give. It was important to us. Three of us could eat for six bucks back then and leave full.

Did we have more than six bucks? Yeah, we did, but we didn't want to eat our "seed." You see, Cathy and I believed our faith was working even when we couldn't see the harvest yet. We knew we were not called to "believing" as some ongoing mental exercise. We were believing as a form of trust in God—and that trust extended not just to what we said, but also to what we did in our everyday life. For us, it felt good to eat cheaper in order to give to causes and people we believed were doing the work of God, and God honored us over and over again.

Why is it so hard for some people to trust God? Why are some so quick to doubt His principles? I believe it is because when some people fail us in life, we tend to think everyone will fail us in life in the end. That is not true. We can't compare God to people because God is not a man that He should lie—and our belief in His Word is a form of trust in Him (Numbers 23:19). We trust in Who He is as not only our Savior, but also our Provider. Belief is a form of trust.

What makes a marriage wonderful? It's not sex. If sex alone made a marriage wonderful, then there wouldn't be so much divorce—because there are a lot of divorced people today that had plenty of sex while they were married. What makes a marriage wonderful is trusting in each other and being honorable to one another, and letting each other know, both in words and in actions, that you love each other enough to be there through the ups and downs of life. There is calm and comfort in living with someone you not only love, but also trust. There's a peace that comes when you know that you're in this life together by choice, and no matter what life throws, you'll always aim to have each other's back.

Doubt Raises Questions That Don't Deserve Answers

There is a verse in the Word that says, *"But foolish and unlearned questions avoid, knowing that they do gender strife"* (2 Timothy 2:23).

Sometimes you have to see that some people use doubt to raise questions that don't deserve answers. If doubt is masquerading as a real question, then see it for what it is. Consider that question "foolish and unlearned." Do what the Word says and avoid all that. We're not called to hotly debate one another and try to prove who's right or wrong when it comes to the Word. When it shifts to just a "who's going to win?" kind of verbal game, opt out. We don't win people to God or to faith through mental gymnastics—we win them through showing them His love, even if we don't agree.

Strife is a disease in the earth and, sadly, it's in the Church, too! What is strife? It's a fruit of the flesh. It's not from God, but a carnal way of being that breeds all sorts of contention. Genesis 13:7 tells us that it's a human problem. Paul echoes that in 1 Corinthians 3:3. Strife is listed alongside things like murder and deceit. It's included with things like jealousy, fits of anger, idolatry, and all sorts of dissensions and divisions (Galatians 5:19-21). The Word warns us that people who do such things won't inherit the kingdom of God—and the kingdom of God is a way of living. It's not the Kingdom of Heaven, which is a place. God's way of *living* is received when we choose His way over our own human nature. It's a better way of living that includes trusting God has our best interest at heart, and avoiding strife.

I believe we can have strife in our own mind when we allow doubt to become a habit—when we don't trust God but instead fight His Word in our own mind. That's being "double-minded," and the Word tells us that flip-flopping this way brings instability to *everything* we do (James 1:8). Remember, when faith is weak, it suspends your judgment—you may have excellent sight but poor perception. Poor choices follow poor perception.

So, when a question comes up that is meant to cast doubt on the goodness of God, I see that doubt as a form of strife—and I don't want to entertain it and let it to lead me into even more strife and instability. I don't want to be wise in knowledge but foolish in deeds. I don't want my actions to match the doubt. I want my mind sound and my faith strong, and I want my actions to match what I believe. You see, I've come to know that not every question needs to be answered, and that some are posed just to breed strife. I don't want to clash with God. I don't want to have conflict in my soul. I don't want to disagree with the God of the Universe! Do you? I'm sure that you don't.

Trust in the Lord. When the devil throws a question meant to cast doubt on the goodness of God in your mind, just tell him, "You answer it, devil." Ignore the foolish and ignorant doubts and just do like Psalm 37:3 says, *"Trust in the Lord, and do good."* Period. Choose faith over all the poor perceptions of doubt.

14

Doubt Is an Unconscious Atheism

I REFUSE TO MAKE MYSELF THE CENTER OF MY OWN BELIEF

Doubting God is a form of pride—it makes you the center of your own belief. Today, the whole world is touting that all you need to do is believe in yourself. I believe in having healthy self-esteem, but our faith is not supposed to be solely in "ourselves." We need God. All you have to do is look around this world to see what happens when people make themselves the center of their own belief, and everything else!

Some people treat God like vitamins: a supplement to whatever they can't get or do on their own—as if God begins where we end, and as if we should only go to Him once we can't do anything for ourselves. But being a believer is about a *relationship* with the Lord that puts Him at the *center* of our lives, not the outskirts.

God doesn't want to just be your "fire insurance" so you don't bust hell wide open. He doesn't want to just be your last-ditch-effort call to Heaven once you've exhausted all other options. God will meet you wherever you are, sure. He will never turn you away no matter what you do. He'll forgive, love, show mercy, and grant you grace—but listen, God wants to be close to you *daily*. He wants fellowship. He is your *Father*. Don't kick your Daddy to the curb.

If We Are the Center of Our Own Belief, Where Does That Place Our Father?

Doubt is a form of pride that puts us at the center of our lives and throws our Heavenly Father to the outskirts. It's more peaceful and effective to have humility and know that we are God's children, not the other way around! If we are the center, then what does that make Him? Relegated to the outside, that's what. A lot of believers treat God like a genie in a lamp and rub on it when they're in trouble, but that is a slap in the face to the God Who loves us and wants a relationship with us.

A person who just tries to use God for what they can get out of Him does it because they live by fear and not faith—they don't realize that their selfish motivations are rooted in a lack mentality. God is our Father and He wants to be a part of our lives. He is a generous Father, but I think it's hurtful to treat Him as if all we need Him for are things. I want to be the kind of person who cares about the Lord and loves Him enough not to treat Him with disrespect. I love God and I love my relationship with Him. That is first place. I also know that if I have childlike faith in Him as my Father, keep Him at the center of my life, and apply His principles the best I know how, He will always richly give me all things to enjoy (1 Timothy 6:17). My faith in *Him* will pull those things that I desire to me like a magnet. I have faith in myself, too, because confidence is a good thing, but my faith is centered on Him way more than it ever is on me.

Sometimes you can turn a verse around to see it in a new light— as in, if nothing is impossible with God, then apparently things are impossible with just man. We need God. We don't just need Him when we're at the end of our rope. We need Him throughout our life, in good times and in challenging times.

It is a joy to develop our relationship with the Lord. It brings peace. It lifts us above what we can do on our own on any given day. His ways are higher than our ways. His thoughts are higher than our thoughts. But, when we have a relationship with Him and spend time understanding His Word, we develop the "mind of Christ" in a way that aligns with His thoughts and ways. Suddenly, we are a success going somewhere to succeed.

God is also a friend beyond compare. Nobody has been a greater friend to me than the Lord. So, why would I want to doubt my friend? Even out of mere loyalty's sake, I would want to believe the best about my friend. God is so far beyond man. He's our Creator, and making Him the center of our heart is just plain in our best interest.

So, our belief must be centered in our Father and not in the people He's created, and that extends to us. As believers, the more we mature in Him, the more we more easily understand the benefits of making Him the center of our belief. Our relationship with God becomes a habitual fellowship that affects our everyday life. It also gives us greater confidence in ourselves. It gives us the boldness to go out and do what He's put on our heart. We aren't meant to just be talkers of the Word, deceiving ourselves with words; we are called to be speakers and doers of the Word (James 1:22). Faith without works is called "dead" for a reason! A "live" faith puts action behind words.

Satan Was a "Forger of His Own Destiny" Outside of God— He Was Gifted, Beautiful, and Talented . . . and Wrong

Satan saw himself as the center of his own belief and the forger of his own destiny *outside* of what God intended him to be. He was given so many great gifts. But pride was Satan's problem. Don't make it yours, too.

Remember that Satan had beauty and talent. He was admired and praised in Heaven, and yet Satan forsook his rightful position in Heaven and forsook the good eternity he was created to enjoy because he chose to make *himself* the center of his own belief instead of God. He convinced a third of Heaven's angels to follow him in that self-centered choice, and since the fall of man, he's been making great efforts to do the same to all of us. So, he may have been gifted, beautiful, and talented, but he was wrong. When we do what he did, that makes us wrong, too.

God is a jealous God when it comes to you. He loves you and wants to be close to you every day. He does not want to share you with the devil. God doesn't want anything coming between you and Him because He knows that without Him, you will go astray.

Satan is a deceiver, and whatever he offers is an attempt to draw you off course and away from the Father. That is Satan's goal—to move you away from God and to steal, kill, and destroy your life in some way (John 10:10).

God is a jealous God, but He is not a selfish God—He is righteous and pure, and He wants the best for His children. He created us, we are His family, and He wants to see all of His children grow, learn, overcome, and succeed in this life and over all the works of the devil, both here and for all of eternity.

We are victorious by the blood of the Lamb (something done for us) and the word of our testimony (using our mouth to declare what has been done for us). Satan hates what Jesus did for us. He wants to shut our mouths from declaring anything good about God, and especially Jesus, Who bruised his head when He went to the cross. Jesus took Satan out at the source—his head! That was the place Satan first rebelled and the place where he planned his revolt against God Almighty. How did he lure the angels away from God? He conjured up doubt in their minds about God.

The battlefield for Satan has always been the mind, which is why it is so critical for us to renew our mind to the Word—this is how we are transformed as people; I can't repeat it enough. Romans 12:2 reminds us, *And be not conformed to this world: but be ye transformed by the renewing of your mind, that ye may prove what is that good, and acceptable, and perfect, will of God.* God doesn't need to have His will proven to Him because He already knows what's in His own mind—it is you and me who need to know, and you and me who need to prove it. We are the ones who prove the perfect and acceptable will of God in our own mind, heart, and life. If we make ourselves the center of our own lives, we're acting like the devil and only proving our own will—we take God completely out of the equation.

Your Time on Earth Is Limited— Make God the Center of Your Belief

I don't care how talented you are, you need God because your heart will seek to fill His space with something. Where your treasure is, there will your heart be also (Matthew 6:12). Your heart longs for God as the centerpoint, even when your mind doesn't realize it, and it will search to fill itself with something, anything, in an effort to calm that craving. Besides, one day you're going to meet your Father face to face—you will have that moment—and you will see clearly that He is the center of all good things anyway.

I don't care how beautiful you are, beauty will not save you. It fades. Have you ever seen a very old person? They were once young. Someone thought they were beautiful, too. Nothing on the outside is worth sacrificing what's on the inside! You can be the most beautiful and celebrated person you know, but guess what? You still need God, because the admiration of others cannot match the self-confidence you get from a close fellowship with the Lord.

You have a limited time on this planet. I know, it may seem long right now—and it may seem especially long if you are struggling in some way. Many people think they have all the time in the world to change or do things differently—they put off drawing close to God thinking they can do it another time. There is no better time than right now. None of us knows the date or the hour when Christ will return any more than we know when we will take our last breath—we don't know those things.

So, it's important to "x out" the prideful thoughts that say, "I'm the center of my own belief" or "I'm enough on my own." All of us will be given moments throughout our life to make that choice—turn to God or turn away from God. Casting down the importance of your Father is just Satan's way of trying to coerce you into turning away. See that for what it is—an attack on your family.

You are part of a divine family. Don't discount God's rightful position as Father in your own life here on earth. That's pride. While it might be tempting to put yourself at the center of your own life, all you have to do is look at the stories in scripture and the world we live in today to see that it doesn't make life better for anyone for very long.

Doubt is a form of pride that puts you at the center of your own belief. It's unconscious atheism. It's like following Satan's lead into misery on earth instead of God's lead into love, joy, peace, health, prosperity, and every other truly good thing in life.

Debt Free Building Project—
I Refused to Put Myself at the Center of My Own Belief

Now, let me show you how I've experienced people trying to make me the center of my own belief in a practical life story. Some people think I'm talented or successful. They praise me for all sorts of things—I always point them to God because I think it's a dangerous thing to believe the praise of others too much. You should never believe your own press! Whether it's great or terrible, it's temporary! Besides, neither matters because you are still you, and God's opinion is what matters most. I've found that you really have to know who you are and also who you are not. Being grounded as a believer is about having yourself firmly planted in God.

But, because some think highly of me, I'm often encountering people who want to make me the center of my own belief. Take our ministry headquarters building project for instance. When I built the ministry headquarters, God told me to do it debt free. I knew it wasn't my own mind and that God had told me to do something impossible. That was His will for not only the buildings but for me. I had to spearhead something I'd never done. I had to have faith for something bigger than I'd ever dreamed of doing. The plans for the headquarters were big and expensive . . . and the plans didn't match what the ministry had in the bank.

My wife, Cathy, and I had the plans drawn up for the entire project, and we were excited. Faith brings a force of energy into your life and all your projects—it's the opposite of bad stress. It's excitement and adventure sometimes, and it's peace and calm at other times. Faith makes you look at the "mountain" and not fear the height. That's sometimes how you know when your belief is moving from God to yourself. When you are overwhelmed with stress about what He's called you to do, it's a sign that you've slipped into the bad habit of making *you* the center of your own belief. When He's the center, it's a much more peaceful place even through the challenges. When fear is gone, obstacles start becoming just one more thing to do—one more thing that you can do with God, because nothing is impossible with God.

Well, everybody Cathy and I told about building our facility debt free thought it couldn't be done. When I'd tell someone about our debt free plan of action or show them the blueprints for the buildings, I was consistently met with a "you can't do that" attitude. I was often told about my own limitations. It almost didn't matter who I was talking to about the buildings—"they" told me it wouldn't work because nobody could build that much debt free. I can't tell you how many times I heard that no ministry or church in Louisiana had built that much debt free before, and that I wouldn't either.

Was I upset with people when they didn't believe? No. God didn't tell *them*; He told me. So, it made sense that they wouldn't grab a hold of the vision as quickly. Was I swayed by their words? No. I didn't let anyone sway me. I figured that God knew more than man, and besides, I already knew that I couldn't do it all on my own, and I was glad—I don't want to be the center of my own belief! I'm confident. I'm bold. But I know who I am, and I'm not God. So, I kept myself in the place He chose for me as His child and decided that I didn't care how long or short it took to complete the project—it was going to be debt free!

Now, I know I live in an economic world, and I never deny what is going on in the world financially. But I do deny the world's right to dictate that I do something *less* when God has told me to do something *more*. So, when I was building the ministry headquarters, I began with paying for one building at a time as the finances came in to do it. God was showing up and showing out, and He began doing that so regularly that I wasn't just building debt free, but I was creating a testimony to other churches of what is possible with God. He was involved in it *all*.

For instance, I had suppliers (that I never asked for a discount), give me metal at cost and roofing at huge discounts, too—everything you can think of that goes into a building, I had some sort of favor surrounding it. Before I knew it, I was building quicker than I imagined and for less money than I'd planned to spend, and God was bringing in extra finances every single month. Offerings were larger. More books and audio messages were being sold. Finances were pouring in from our Partners, and we were gaining new Partners every day, too. Cathy and I were literally watching God do a miracle nearly every day in our ministry finances and with suppliers in order to bring to pass the thing He had told us to believe and to do.

Now, God had told me at the very beginning of the project that when I was 80 percent finished with one building to pour the slab for the next one, and so on. So, before I knew it, I had finished building one and poured the slab for building two. It was amazing in my eyes and in everyone else's who saw it and knew that it was all happening debt free to the glory of God.

Some People Don't Lack Faith in Themselves or God, but They Do Lack Faith in *Your* Choice to Make God the Center

When I look back now, I see so clearly how the root of everybody's disbelief was that they were making *me* the center of the project. They were looking at what *I* could do on my own and also just relying on what other churches and ministries had done in their building projects. Before we broke ground on the first building, I had three banks approach me to loan the ministry money for the whole project.

Whitney Bank, First American Bank, and Hibernia Bank wanted the ministry's business and were offering great rates, but each one told me the same thing as everyone else—that I couldn't build that much debt free. They told me I didn't have enough money, but I told them they didn't have enough faith. They thought building debt free was impossible, and guess what? They were right. What they didn't know was that God wasn't looking at what *I* could do; He was looking at what *He* could do if I'd just have the gall and audacity to believe and obey. That's all God asked me to do.

You see, sometimes people don't lack faith in themselves, and sometimes they don't lack faith in God either, but they do lack faith in *you*. I now see that all the naysayers were trying to convince me of one thing: to put myself at the center of my own belief. They didn't see the ministry as God's so much as they saw it as mine alone, and as such, they were trying to get me to see the truth of my own limitations. They were trying to infect me with doubt in what *I* could do. I don't think anybody directly meant to do that. I don't think they even realized it. But, every time they told me "you can't," that is exactly what they were saying. Well, I already knew I couldn't! And I also already knew that God could!

Cathy and I were excited for the adventure of building in faith. I have to say that my wife has always stood with me in faith for whatever the ministry needed or whatever God put on my heart for His ministry. Together, we've seen God do so many impossible things that it is very hard to sway us. We're a united front, and we know that God does miracles.

There's No Way I Could Have Done It—I'm Not That Good!

Today, it's been many years since our ministry headquarters were built, and I'm honored and blessed to say that we did it all debt free to the glory of God. Do you realize the savings of building that way? They told me I would have paid $20 million in interest over the years if I'd taken out the 30-year loan!

I'm so proud to say that there is not one thing built on our ministry grounds that is *not* debt free. Nothing has a note from the bank attached to it. There is no interest paid on a loan of any kind on any building or piece of equipment at our ministry. Now, I'm a decent guest speaker, but there is no way I could have done that. I'm not that good! Everything I see at our headquarters is a financial miracle from God, and I know without a shadow of a doubt that it NEVER would have happened if I had made myself the center of my own belief.

God must be first in all areas, but especially when you are believing to do impossible things in your life. Don't let doubt make you the center of your own belief. Have childlike faith and be aware of the importance of obeying God's voice, and you will see His mighty hand move in your life in ways you never could have done if you were trying to do it all on your own.

Satan Is God's Enemy, and He Can't Give What He *Was*; He Can Only Give What He Has *Become*

Do you ever wonder what mankind would be doing right now if Adam and Eve had made the choice to follow God's best for their lives? We would all be living entirely differently here on this planet. Eden was a paradise for mankind, and it was God's will that it be that way—it was permeated by His will and His truth. The choice to pick *greater knowledge* over God's will and truth changed everything.

Let's go back to the author of doubt again. Lucifer was called Light-Bearer and the Morning Star *before* he rebelled. He has been called many names since then, such as the Serpent, the Dragon, the Father of Lies, the Adversary, the Accuser, the Evil One, the Tempter, and more. All of his names are negative, except the ones before the fall of man. Now, these "names" give us a heads-up over and over to remind us of his character—to remind us what we are dealing with. Still, our focus isn't supposed to be on God's enemy but on God Himself. When we realize that all the evil that exists in the world comes from God's enemy, we are able to see all the works of the devil as having their foundation in pride and self-centeredness.

Rebellion against God's will and truth begins subtly—when we choose to put ourselves and our thoughts above His. It can begin by choosing to doubt God's character or pass judgment on God's words or ways. When we put ourselves in the judgment seat of God Himself and start saying what we don't like, we are falling into a trap. God is God. We are not. Doubting His good character in little areas of life can mushroom and, in the end, become a rebellion. Believers who decide not to believe often started out simply putting themselves at the center of their own belief.

There is a marked difference in people who follow God's truth verses those who follow the twisted ways of the devil. Satan's lies don't come out of the blue; they come from the world we live in—he isn't called the god of this age, the ruler of this world, and the prince of the power of the air for nothing!

The term "the devil" is used in the Word not just as God's enemy's name, but it's tied to anything that stands in opposition to God and His plan. He's the first murderer. In convincing Eve and Adam that he'd give them the light of knowledge, he effectively killed them two ways that day—first, the separation from God was instant (a spiritual death) and second, the body began to die then, too (a physical death would come, as it would eventually wear out).

Never forget that he still thinks of himself as "Light-Bearer"—one of his deceiving tactics is to shine a light on some area he thinks a person will agree with that goes *against* God's Word. Just remember that he's not a light-bearer anymore. He's a liar, an accuser, a tempter, and an adversary to truth. He is just posing as his former self when he tries to enlighten someone against God. His end game is always stealing, killing, or destroying someone or something.

Satan can't give mankind what he *was*. He can only give what he has *become*. He was a light-bearer, but now he can only give darkness disguised as enlightenment. Because he's a liar, he easily exchanges truth for lies. He twists the truth and twists the minds of people, too. He can make even the vilest things look "good" in the eyes of those he deceives. His goal is to hurt God by hurting His creation.

Many people today have been deceived into thinking they have seen the light when they speak *against* God's truth. Today, so many have believed the Liar's lies that they openly show hatred and disgust for the Word of God and those who follow the Lord. This is how things can become upside down in the world. When what is good is called wrong in the world and when darkness becomes celebrated, you know you are seeing the work of God's enemy in action!

Power is tempting for people, and the devil knows it, so he often tempts people to place themselves at the center of their own lives. They become selfish and uncaring about others, and smug about the leadership of God. They can become haters of truth because they prefer the lies. But no matter how subtly he deceives people in the beginning by trying to appeal to the desire for power or knowledge, he always ends up acting and drawing people to act in accordance with *his* true nature.

The devil is not a faith devil; he's a flesh devil. A person doesn't sin without first being tempted in the flesh. Nobody is tempted by God's enemy to do what is right unless it's just for show—a way to cover the true intent to do wrong. When a person poses as good but commits great evil, they have been greatly deceived by God's enemy. Today, we are seeing some actually celebrate what we instinctively know is wrong so much that they call it "good." Now, that's twisted!

God is very clear about what is right and wrong, and He has even written this on our own heart. The temptation to *not* be clear about right and wrong is rooted in Satan's own confusion—he is called the author of confusion for a reason, and he is the twister of minds. In believers, that twisting begins with the idea that God's truth is presumptuous, unreasonable, and undoable. This is a bald-faced lie. Don't let the lies of the devil make you think you aren't capable of using God's Word to see success in your life—because you most certainly are!

Not Understanding Isn't a Reason to Doubt God

Doubt undermines the foundation of Christianity because it produces a religion instead of a relationship. The Church gave up the miraculous in favor of doubt when it decided to play church and not believe. Many teach that God puts sickness on people to teach them something, and yet Jesus never did that—He didn't go around putting sickness on people. No, He is the Healer. He's called the Great Physician.

Sometimes people don't receive healing here on earth, and then others are left with a lack of understanding as to why. I've found that just because you don't understand something doesn't mean you should call God a liar—it doesn't mean you should abandon your hope or your trust in His goodness. You just have to be honest enough to tell God when you don't understand. Let His Holy Spirit guide you. Believe His Word that says He will liberally give you wisdom when you ask for it. Choose trust, even if you don't understand a situation, knowing that trusting God brings peace to your soul.

When I read Isaiah 53:5, *"But He was wounded for our transgressions, He was bruised for our iniquities: the chastisement of our peace was upon Him; and with His stripes we are healed,"* I don't have to understand all the intricacies of the spiritual work of the cross to simply trust that this is what God's Word says Jesus did for us. I trust that God is God. I trust that He is not a liar. So, my trust in Him fuels my belief that I can be healed by believing in the stripes laid on Jesus' back.

So, when somebody talks to me about healing and says, "Well, you know how God is. Sometimes He does and sometimes He don't!" I don't accept it because that is doubting God. I may not understand why one manifested healing and another didn't, but I don't accuse

God of not holding up His end. Nobody put me as judge over God Almighty. I'm not about to cut Him down just because I don't understand something—I know in my heart that if there is a problem, it is not with God. He is not a man that He can lie. If He says His covenant will He not break nor alter the things that have gone out of His lips (Psalm 89:34), then that is the way it is!

I hope I'm making sense here. I pray you are getting this because when you make it more black and white and less gray, you will have *much* better results. Religion is filled with gray thinking. It's filled with loopholes that make doubt seem pious. If doubt itself could be canonized, the Church would have made it a saint by now—it's that revered, even though it's totally wrong. There is a lot of unconscious atheism in religion! Many things are truthfully stated because people believe them, but they aren't statements of truth.

Jesus also raised people from the dead. Jesus couldn't go to funerals because He'd mess them up. Even His most loyal followers had a hard time believing that Jesus could raise people from the dead, but He did it. The only times Jesus could do no mighty works is when nobody believed. You see, faith in the heart of the individual has always been tied to the mighty works of Christ. Jesus wasn't a magician. He was more of a conduit for our faith.

The Word tells us to fight the good fight of faith, but it doesn't tell us to fight faith itself. Many people dealing with sickness are fighting for their faith mentally while their body is trying to fight physically. But you can't convince yourself to believe when you don't trust God in the first place.

Many die "in faith" and that doesn't negate the truth that faith is what heals. It also doesn't make them bad people at all, or even weak people—it just means there was a disconnect between their heart, mind, and the words of God. We may not know what the disconnect is for them, but God knows—and He loves them with an undying love, and is on the other side of this life waiting to welcome every believer home. We also don't always have to have an answer if someone doesn't receive their healing and goes home to be with the Lord "in faith." I find many people will say just about *anything* in order to give an "answer" to something they can't admit to not understanding.

The Secret Things Belong to the Lord—
Never Condemn Another for a "Lack of Faith"

The Word tells us that, *"The secret things belong unto the Lord our God: but those things which are revealed belong to us and to our children for ever, that we may do all the words of this law"* (Deuteronomy 29:29). So, there are some "secret things" that only belong to the Lord—and until you cross over, you may never know "why" someone you love didn't receive their healing here on earth. Be assured, though, they received it the moment they crossed over!

Never condemn a believer for not receiving from God. Never condemn what you see as a "lack of faith"—if you see someone sick and having a hard time receiving, don't speak evil words cloaked in religion. If you've got so much faith, produce it. And if you can't, then trust God and pray for them as you show them great love. Remember, Romans 8:1 tells us that there is no condemnation for those who are in Christ Jesus—and so, if God Himself doesn't condemn a believer, who are we to do it? God has called us to love people. We love them through their strengths and their weaknesses, just as we would want them to do with us.

Remember, just because we may not know the secret things, or just because we do not know where the disconnect lies doesn't mean that God is untruthful. He is not a liar just because we don't understand something. We can pray for Him to reveal reasons or we can simply let go, trusting that even if we don't have all the answers, He does—and just as our loved one is safe in His care, our heart is safe in His care, too. We can be content in all situations knowing that He never leaves us or forsakes us (Hebrews 13:5).

The Heart of Man Is Complex, and God Knows Every Part of It

I've been a minister for so many years. I've seen many people who were believing God for their healing outwardly, but just at the end of their life told me otherwise. Sometimes people hide in their heart what they really believe or even really want. Many will tell me they are tired and ready to go, even as their children are praying for them to live.

The will of a person is very strong. Death and life are in the power of the tongue. Some people who love God know so clearly where they are going that it actually inhibits their desire to fight the good fight of faith—they begin to let go in their mind before they ever tell their family. I've seen that a lot, too.

The heart of man is complex, and God knows every bit of it. We shouldn't indulge in unconscious atheism by saying God and His Word aren't true just because we don't know the ins and outs of another person's belief. We can't know the heart of man like God can. Doing so is just like mimicking Satan in the Garden with Eve, "Hath God said?"—questioning God's Word or His motives as pure is similar to questioning His existence in your life as God.

Don't fall into an unconscious atheism by indulging doubt. It may have been "unconscious" to you before, but I hope you begin to catch yourself and make a conscious choice to simply believe God anyway today—even if it takes a bit for your understanding to catch up to your faith. I hope you see that making God the center of your belief is always the right way to go.

Doubt Is a Low Morale of the Heart

IT LEADS US TO THINK GOD'S TRUTH IS PRESUMPTUOUS AND UNREASONABLE

When I got saved after hearing the message of salvation on television and asking God to come into my life, my eyes were opened. I turned the light on when I let the Light of the world into my heart, and suddenly it was like scales fell off of my eyes. A reversal of how I saw the world around me began to occur. What I used to see as good, I began to see more clearly as not good at all.

I was under contract and I had to play music at a nightclub right after I got born again. I remember going into the club and seeing it so differently. I used to think it was great; there was nowhere I wanted to be more than at one of the shows. But then I looked around and it looked like a velvet-lined sewer. The lifestyle I used to love and live for without even thinking suddenly became repulsive to me because I could actually discern it for what it was.

So, when Christians warned me that I'd be tempted to go back, I thought that was a joke. Why would I *ever* go back to that darkness that Jesus saved me from? What was there to go back to? NOTHING good. God saved me from misery, and there was no way I was going back to where I was before. There is a scripture that says, *"As a dog returneth to his vomit, so a fool returneth to his folly"* (Proverbs 26:11)—and that's exactly how I began to think about it. You see, it's not until the light comes that you can see the foulness of the darkness.

I've seen many believers lately begin to see the darkness as "less dark" than they used to. I've notice that it always begins with some doubt about God's truth—but the reality is that the more you accept the little lies of the enemy, the less they sound like lies at all. But they are lies, make no mistake. This is how doubt can draw you back to a place you once were delivered from—and it's damaging for your heart because it is like binding yourself in tight chains when God created you to live open and free.

The scripture "as a dog returns to his own vomit so a fool returns to his folly" is a pretty accurate description to me. Doubt is folly. Trust and faith lift the heart, but doubt creates bad morale. Doubt clouds the heart with worries that should never be there. But God's Word and spending time with Him can bust through all that.

You're a Light Shining in the Darkness, and Doubt Just Dulls Your Shine

Doubt is low morale of the heart—it steals your ambition to pursue goodness and truth. It causes people to not even try. Some think God's truth is presumptuous and unreasonable, even if they won't admit it aloud. They are so beat down by listening to the world 24/7 that they look at God's Word and think they can't do it anyway, so why bother trying? That train of thought is just darkness going to seed—and the world has enough darkness already. Remember that we are the light of the world, and we can't shine if we are defeated in our own mind. All doubt does is dull our shine.

Defeatism will always just perpetuate more of the same. It'll just create more doom and gloom in the mind. God's ability to save and teach His children to live well is proven by millions of believers every day who live by faith and do great things in this world. They may not get the press, but God sees every single moment—and each act of faith is a light shining in the darkness.

If you're a believer and you're low on faith and joy, it's usually just because you've been hearing the wrong things too much—you've been diving into darkness more than light. Reverse your hearing-habits, and push the light instead of the doubtful darkness. Then, the light of God will rise up and help you push away the doom and gloom. Think about it: When you turn a light on in a dark room, what happens? Darkness flees! The moment the light starts being allowed to shine, it's a deterrent for the dark, and that includes thoughts.

Some people see so much that they start to falsely assume that it's just human nature to do wrong—but that's not true once you are a believer. If you think the blood of the Lamb and the word of our testimony can't overcome human nature, you are entertaining doubt about God's ability to change the heart of a person. You are deceived. You're saying that Satan is more powerful than God, and that's a lie.

God can change anybody who will seek Him. Whatever we seek in faith, that's what we find—so as a believer, we should seek God if we want to be godlier. You see, no matter what lies the world may tell you, as a believer, you can overcome the darkness. Every time you seek to draw close to Him, every time you have faith in His Word, and every day you go out and make good choices—which are God-choices— you are pushing the light. That changes not only your mindset for the better, but it also changes the situations you are in for the better.

Don't let the darkness of the world drag you down. Let it flow right on out. Choose to be free of that doom and gloom mentality, even if you see a lot of darkness in this world. Just because you see it doesn't mean it has to drag you down into the same dark place. You can see the darkness for what it is and still be at peace when you realize that the light of God is always accessible, and all you need is a small spark of it to make a difference.

Living According to the Light Is the Best Life, but All the Works of the Devil Are Unreasonable and Presumptuous

I didn't get saved just to follow some moral code of ethics; I got saved to be free and to have a relationship with the One Who made me. The longer I'm saved, the more I see that His way of living is the only reasonable way to live—it's true freedom from the spirit outward. The light of God's Spirit is easy to recognize. Love, joy, peace, patience, kindness, goodness, faithfulness, gentleness, and self-control—these are the fruit of God's Spirit, and it's what we exude when His light is burning bright in us.

Jesus is the Vine, and we are the branches, and we're supposed to be dropping the fruit of the Spirit everywhere we go. That's the good life, and it's good any way you look at it! You can have everything the world offers and be rich materially, but if you're without God, you've got soul poverty. The riches of this world cannot compare to the riches of grace found in Christ Jesus—but don't think that just because you find God that poverty must be next, because that's not true no matter what religiosity says.

Remember that it's God Who gives us richly all things to enjoy. It's God Who gives us riches with no sorrow attached. It's God Who will bless us in the city, in the field, coming in, and going out. God's blessing on our life starts spiritually and permeates our soul (mind, will, emotions) to the degree that we so let His light shine—and every principle He has leads to a better life, which affects us spiritually, physically, *and* financially. God is concerned about it *all*.

Once we accept God's plan of salvation through His Son's death, burial, and resurrection on the cross, we change *instantly* in the spirit—the light comes on inside of us and we have access to new sight. What we couldn't understand before because we were spiritually dead to God, we suddenly gain the ability to understand. After being saved a while, some Christians let the author of confusion creep back in, and they start listening to his lies about God's truth—that it's unreasonable and presumptuous. But the truth is that Satan is unreasonable. Satan is presumptuous.

The god of this world exchanges right for wrong every chance he can get away with, and the Word tells us in Revelation 12:12 that he'll do it more and more as he perceives the day approaching when Jesus will come back. In his last-ditch effort to gain more away from God, he will make the things God calls wrong "right" in the sight of the world. So, we need the light burning bright within us so we don't fall for it. Being a believer isn't just about some mindset shift; it's a spiritual rebirth we undergo upon salvation, and that rebirth gives us access to see through the lies. The natural man doesn't understand the things of the Spirit—they're foolishness to Him—but the spiritual man *does* understand (1 Corinthians 2:14).

Even if you just got saved today, your eyes see clearer than yesterday. After your rebirth, you begin the process of renewing your mind to the Word so that you can more accurately discern spiritual things—and like a baby who starts learning to crawl, it's not long before you're walking and running in the light. All of us fall short of the glory of God, but the goal is to remember that when we fall, we shall arise—because we're God's children, we are growing, and the devil is no match for Who lives within us.

God can help us to overcome ALL the works of the devil that pop up as we move through our day. He can open our eyes to see what's really going on so we can pray, believe, and sidestep the lies. We've got a built-in Adviser that can guide us day by day, and I don't know about you, but that lifts my morale—that gives me ambition to stir up the gift of God's Spirit in my life every day. I don't want to miss an opportunity to be lifted up and shone the right way—to be filled with more of His glorious light.

We Were Created to Follow God's Lead— Our Spirit Longs to Be Led by His Truth and Love

Each day we have choices—will we do what's right? Will we act in love? Will we let the light show us where the dark spots are in our everyday life? Ultimately, will we take our rightful place as light-spreaders? Will we love God with all our heart, mind, and soul? Will we love His Word, even if it seems hard by comparison to the easy temptations of this world? Will we rise up with Him or fall down with the devil? Will we say "no" to the devil when he comes slithering in subtly with doubt and say "yes" to the God Who created paradise for us to enjoy?

"And God blessed them, and God said unto them, Be fruitful, and multiply, and replenish the earth, and subdue it . . ."—these words in Genesis 1:28 are a guide for how to live and govern the earth. We must be fruitful with the good things God's given us. It's our job to multiply what's good. If we take something from this earth, it's our job to replenish whatever has been taken. And it's our job to subdue whatever rises up against God and us, which means to have dominion over the place God gave us. We can be good rulers of our lives or bad rulers of our lives; it is up to us!

Never forget that YOU have authority over the devil and all his works. The Word is called the sword of the Spirit for a reason. It is a weapon against the *spiritual* powers that continually try to twist and warp the way God meant for this world to be—so the Word is something you want to use. The powers and principalities of the air are subdued when we speak God's Word because His anointing is on His Word.

If one third of Heaven fell with Satan, that means there are a lot of fallen angels inhabiting the air and everywhere outside of Heaven. This is why we speak the Word and fill the air with the truth! The sword of the Spirit fights what we cannot see, but that still affects the world. We don't fixate on the darkness; we simply speak what God says, push the light, and move on! Why waste time with the devil when you could be creating some heaven right here on earth with the Words of God?

Heaven is where God rules, and it's our final destination. There is no poverty, sickness and disease, or misery and mayhem in Heaven because God rules there. This world is a temporary thing, and it's run by the devil. The works of the devil are done every day. Even if we've been lied to and trained from birth to adapt to the way the god of this world runs the earth, once we are rebirthed through salvation, we stop accepting this world "as it is"—and our spirit instinctively seeks to change the world with God's love. What begins in us is meant to flow out to others. We become givers because we serve the Ultimate Giver, Who gave His Son for us.

We suddenly don't want others living in the dark. We want to shine the light of the Gospel, and that's a wonderful thing. The evangelistic desire is motivated by love for all of humanity—by seeing people like Jesus saw them, as lost sheep in need of a Good Shepherd, we naturally want to give what we've been given at a spiritual level.

You see, we are going to be led by someone or something. We were created to follow God and be led by His love. So, people will always look to be led. That's not bad, but it goes south really quickly when people are continually living their lives led by the god of this world!

I Don't Get in the Ditch to Fight the Devil—I Am Seated in High Places with Christ Jesus and Win from There!

Since the god of this world doesn't lead us, we recognize his tactics and games. Satan has no new tricks. He's still stealing, killing, and destroying. He's always trying to bring his false version of "light" one way or another, too.

Just like in the Garden, when he tempted Eve by telling her he'd help her to know more, see more, and experience more in order to be more like God, he will always tempt man with those same temptations. And those temptations, if chosen, will *always* lead God's children away from their Father. The devil has been a breaker of families from the beginning.

The devil is a false light-bringer, and his version of "enlightenment" will always, in the end, bring us to doubt God's goodness, doubt God's love, doubt God's Word, and doubt God's ways. Doubt is always going to factor in, without a doubt! The Word tells us in 2 Corinthians 11:13-15 that he will try to come as an angel of light, but he isn't light—that's false light. There isn't one good thing left in Satan, and there is zero truth in him either. He's a slanderer, a deceiver, and is always ruthless in the end no matter how mild he begins. He's not above twisting scripture to get people to exchange truth for lies and feel good about it.

The easiest way I've found to beat the devil's game is to just place my faith in God and His Word—to move my focus to what matters, which is Jesus. I don't get in the ditch to fight the devil. God's Word said in Ephesians 2:5-6 that by grace I've been saved, and because of that, God raised me up together with Jesus and made me to sit in heavenly places with Christ. So, I'd say that I don't have to get down in the mud and sling it! I don't have to "fight the devil"—I fight for my faith. The good fight of faith is about faith, it's not about fighting the devil.

The god of this world is an idiot. I'm not rebelling against God along with him. I rise above him; I don't cower beneath him. I don't worry about the one who can try and harm me here because with Christ, I will overcome—I care about the One Who made me and has my soul in His care. I serve God. So, like Ephesians says, I see myself seated with Christ in heavenly places. I see myself in that high place and let God's victory be mine instead of going to the low places with the devil. I have chosen not to lean on my own understanding but put my trust in the Lord. If a thought comes up that's against God, I put it down quickly. I don't rehearse those thoughts; I replace them with the truth. This is how I never "learned" to doubt.

Refusing to "Learn" to Doubt—
It's the Best Thing You Can Do for Yourself

God is the only True God. The ruler of this world doesn't come close— all the "gods" that ever were aren't God, and they pale in comparison. They are false representatives of light and twisters of truth. I personally believe that the reason God gave us the ability to doubt in the first place was so that we could doubt *them!*

Ephesians is my favorite book in the Bible, and I want you to read the entire chapter two—to see the wonderful work God has done, and why you no longer have to identify with the world or the ways of the world. The higher life is *for* you because the pure shed blood of Jesus purchased it for you and ALL who have the guts and desire to call upon His name.

> And you hath He quickened, who were dead in trespasses and sins;
> Wherein in time past ye walked according to the course of this world, according to the prince of the power of the air, the spirit that now worketh in the children of disobedience:
> Among whom also we all had our conversation in times past in the lusts of our flesh, fulfilling the desires of the flesh and of the mind; and were by nature the children of wrath, even as others.
> But God, Who is rich in mercy, for His great love wherewith He loved us,
> Even when we were dead in sins, hath quickened us together with Christ, (by grace ye are saved;)
> And hath raised us up together, and made us sit together in heavenly places in Christ Jesus:
> That in the ages to come He might shew the exceeding riches of His grace in His kindness toward us through Christ Jesus.
> For by grace are ye saved through faith; and that not of yourselves: it is the gift of God:

Not of works, lest any man should boast.

For we are His workmanship, created in Christ Jesus unto good works, which God hath before ordained that we should walk in them.

Wherefore remember, that ye being in time past Gentiles in the flesh, who are called Uncircumcision by that which is called the Circumcision in the flesh made by hands;

That at that time ye were without Christ, being aliens from the commonwealth of Israel, and strangers from the covenants of promise, having no hope, and without God in the world:

But now in Christ Jesus ye who sometimes were far off are made nigh by the blood of Christ.

For He is our peace, Who hath made both one, and hath broken down the middle wall of partition between us;

Having abolished in His flesh the enmity, even the law of commandments contained in ordinances; for to make in Himself of twain one new man, so making peace;

And that He might reconcile both unto God in one body by the cross, having slain the enmity thereby:

And came and preached peace to you which were afar off, and to them that were nigh.

For through Him we both have access by one Spirit unto the Father.

Now therefore ye are no more strangers and foreigners, but fellow-citizens with the saints, and of the household of God;

And are built upon the foundation of the apostles and prophets, Jesus Christ Himself being the chief corner stone;

In Whom all the building fitly framed together groweth unto an holy temple in the Lord:

In Whom ye also are builded together for an habitation of God through the Spirit.

EPHESIANS 2:1-22

We are brothers and sisters—fellow citizens of the household of God. That means we live here, but we aren't from here anymore. Together, *we* are the temple of God on this earth. Notice how there's no doubt in those verses. Notice how much unity is in those verses. You see, when we let go of doubt and find God through Christ, we find ourselves—and when we are at peace with God and ourselves, we are called then to be at peace with others. It's not much trouble to be at peace with others if you are at peace with God and yourself.

Doubting God Is a Gateway to Misery; Jesus Is the Gateway to Peace

Doubting God is a gateway to misery. But trusting in Him and what He has done through the work of Jesus is a gateway to peace. Doubt tore us from God in the Garden ages ago, but faith is what restores us to God any day of the week. We become something new individually when we get saved, but it's *together* where we really shine. This is why the devil fights the Church so much. Unity is our power in a way that Satan knows he cannot come close to matching.

Those last few verses we just read in Ephesians chapter two show how that, together, we become something only God could envision—a human "holy temple" on this earth. It's not just built; it grows! Like a baby grows into a mature adult, the body of Christ grows into a holy temple that God chooses to reside within.

Our foundations are the apostles and the prophets. Jesus Himself is the chief corner stone. But ALL of us who are reborn and choose the light of God are a part of this great and magnificent human holy temple—and we are powerful together. God sees every person. Every person makes the temple what it is. The spiritual house of God on this planet began the moment Jesus came.

What did Jesus say about us? Read Matthew 16:16-19 and see that Jesus said the gates of hell would not prevail against the Church—this "holy temple" of humans has been building since Jesus came, and it's the place where God resides on the earth. He is in us, and together we give Him a place to be that has power over all the works of the devil.

Jesus said He's given us the keys to the kingdom—it's this truth that helps us bind and loose things in the spirit. And all of us who believe and have taken up the cross to follow Christ have a place and part to play. Even if we are alone, we have power with God. But when we stand together in the unity of our faith—notice I didn't say doctrine—it is our unified faith that expands the temple and gives God more place on this earth.

God made us social beings for a reason. We were created to be a family, and not a distant one, but one that connects because we are already connected deeply. Together, we are built into something beautiful that is God's own place, and together we are so powerful that even hell itself cannot conquer us. We are God's people, temples in His sight. We are the body of Christ. We are the Church that the gates of hell can't prevail against. The more we doubt God, the more we will doubt ourselves and undermine this truth—the truth about who we *are*!

Faith builds what no devil in hell can change or twist. Faith makes us like children again. Faith brings joy that is hard to understand, even if the devil is raging in the world around us. Faith shines a light in the darkness. Faith brings a hope that lights fires in people for goodness. Faith refuses the darkness of strife and creates a path for peace—the path starts in us individually, but we walk it out as a giant family.

We're a living people who follow the Living God. Life is for living, not surviving. And when we choose to let go of doubt, we give ourselves room to reach out in the faith we need to live blessed—spiritually, physically, financially, and in every relationship God brings upon our path.

God's will for us is good. Is our will for us good, too? Each of us has to decide that for ourselves—but it sure makes the choice easier when we draw close to the light of God and let it shine a light on our path. Life is sweeter and easier on the heart when we choose to avoid the low morale of the heart that is *doubt*.

16

Children Are Born Believers

IT'S TIME FOR YOU TO GO BACK IN TIME

My granddaughter's name is Meredith. When she was little, her favorite animated character was Tinker Bell's sister—a white-headed little fairy with wings called Periwinkle. She used to tell me she loved "Peri" because, "She has hair like you, Grandfather." Now, I don't watch cartoons, but I suddenly liked Periwinkle a whole lot. I wanted to buy my granddaughter the whole Disney Store as thanks!

Meredith loved fantasy cartoons, but as a kid, I was less into that sort of thing. Even in the TV shows I liked, they were more grounded in what I thought was reality. That meant I liked western gunslingers or even the mafia shows—anything I thought actually existed. Because of how I was raised, I learned very early in life that unless you had a grip on reality, you weren't going to make it! I learned too early that the world is tough, and so tough guys are what I tended to like best in TV shows and movies.

As a kid, I was freaked out by the supernatural. I remember watching Dracula on TV, even though my mama told me not to watch it—and all night I couldn't sleep a wink. I kept saying "Jesus!" over and over again. I was keeping my brother, Wayne, up all night with me, and finally he had enough and did something he didn't often do. He called Mama for help. My mama was a Pentecostal by that point, and she told me I needed to combat the fear of Dracula by "pleading the blood of Jesus" over my mind. That freaked me out even worse than the movie. I said, "No, Mama! He likes blood! He likes blood!!!" She laughed, but I was serious. I didn't want anybody taking my blood! I had childlike faith that what Dracula *said* he would do, he *would* do—and he'd do to me!

Children are funny. They are born believers. Meredith could sit and play for hours with those little plastic dolls. She could look at them and see what I couldn't see as an adult—she could see the pixies fly. When I was a kid, I could play with a little matchbox car for hours. I could zoom it in the air and see what no adult around me could see—I could see them drive on air, just flying on roads that nobody but me could see. Children are born believers. Until you teach them to doubt, either directly or indirectly, they easily believe. Jesus taught that we should go back and aim for childlike faith in God. In other words, the pure heart we had as children is meant to be the faith lifestyle of believers.

We Were Created from the Breath of God and from the Dust of the Earth Before Sin

Doubt produced sin in the beginning, and with our choice to sin, we stole our right to remain in paradise—but I believe that mankind holds a memory of a time without sin, and perhaps it is why so many dream of utopia here on earth. It's one of the reasons why we fight against the *effects* of the fall of man so much. We don't want to be sick, because in our deep collective memory, we remember that the body was not made to be diseased and die. We don't want to be in dire poverty, because in our collective memory, we remember when there was only abundance, more than enough for all needs and desires, and there just was no such thing as lack.

We were made from the breath of God and the dust of the earth—and the earth at that time of our creation was one without the effects of sin. So, our body fights death with all it's got. We hate poverty and misery; we hope for less drama and stress. In fact, in life, whenever we see injustice or wrongs done, something in our soul fights against it because we know deep inside we were never created to experience those things. We know they are not natural to our origin.

Down through the generations, I believe sin kept compounding and further ruining everything—leaving trails of unbelief, misery, and all types of abuse to the human body, soul, and spirit. Today, we have the idea that sin is just "human nature," but it's not. The purity and innocence of a baby is the closest thing we have to see what human nature was really intended to be—and it's wonderful. This is why when we hear of or see people abusing children, we collectively know it's not only wrong but also evil to do damage to something so fresh, new, open, and full of wonder. It's why when we see the perpetrator, we know they are motivated by evil selfishness.

We Weren't Created to Just Survive, We Were Created to Have Life in Abundance

You were born with faith. You were born with wonder. You were born with an imagination that is probably one of the closest things to faith the natural man has in this life. Hope is in the heart of a child, unless that child's hopes are crushed—and many of us have had our hopes crushed early on in life.

I had all my hopes and dreams crushed pretty young. I was constantly told what I couldn't be or couldn't have. I was called stupid often. I wasn't given much love, and I didn't have much hope. I didn't think I could trust anybody, and I proved myself right. I learned to focus on reality and what I could do on my own; I didn't think I had the luxury of fantasy or even dreaming. I chose to be calculating in making something of myself and to be ambitious.

When I found the Lord, I had already accomplished what I set out to do in life. I had what I thought I wanted, but I wasn't happy because the life I was living was without hope. My salvation lifted the weight of not only sin off my heart, but it also lifted the weight of the struggle of living life without faith in God, without peace, and without childlike wonder. When we accept Jesus, we are really going back to our original state of mind—except it's not automatic anymore; it's a choice we make. Staying close to God, that choice becomes easier and easier as we renew our mind to what He says in His Word. We begin the process of not just undoing the lies but replacing those lies with the truth. The Holy Spirit helps us as He guides us into all truth.

Childlike faith is what Jesus told us to aspire to—and I think it paints a pretty clear picture of how we as God's children are supposed to believe. Wonderment marks the life of children until they are taught differently or see too much that they shouldn't see. Questioning is part of the human brain—we want to both dream and figure things out. Yet, when children question, they do it out of pure curiosity and wonder. They don't question an adult out of doubt, unless they've already been taught to doubt—they don't begin with a mindset that someone is always looking to lie to them, harm them, or deceive them out of something good. Many adults question God in that harmful mindset they learned as children in a fallen world, where adults disappointed them time and time again.

From Survival Mode to Childlike Faith, Regardless of Where You Started

How do we teach our kids to doubt? We teach them with what we say and what we do; what we allow and what we condemn. They learn love or hate by looking at everyone who they come into contact with. They learn trust or distrust that way, too. Every time they are offered something and then it's pulled away, they learn to doubt the hand coming toward them. Every time they are mistreated, they learn to doubt the motives and intentions of others. How disappointments are handled by adults is how a child will learn to think about life in general, and it will affect that person all of their life unless they find the truth and let go of the lies.

Many adults today are really just grown-up used and abused children who were rarely if ever treated right, and they are still in survival mode. When we come to Christ and begin living by faith and not by sight, we begin learning how to really live. Many have learned how to survive in life, but just because we learn to survive through difficulty doesn't mean we know how to really *live* and make our lives great. Survival is not God's best.

Living by faith and not by sight is a Christian concept based on the Word, and it requires that we go back in time, so to speak. To understand childlike faith is to revisit a childhood we may never have even had—but our spirit knows what "should have been," and in Christ we learn to live as new creatures. The term "born again" means we have a fresh start in God. We go back to our origin in God; we leave the sin to disintegrate in the righteousness of the blood of Jesus, Who was sinless when He paid the price for us. His sacrifice cancels out all of our sin and gives us a fresh start.

So, even if you have never experienced or don't ever remember experiencing childlike faith as a child because of your upbringing, I want you to know that inside of you exists a collective human memory of a time when there was *no* sin—and mankind walked in the cool of the day with God, who was Someone they knew was full of love and could be trusted. This is what the soul longs to experience again, and it's why we get so irritated at the evils in the world, even if we've come to see them as "normal." They may be normal, but they aren't right. Love is right. Peace is right. Goodness and mercy are right. I don't care what you saw as a kid, when you walk in the light, you walk in what's right.

Twin Brothers Two Ways—
Sin and Unbelief, Righteousness and Faith

Sin and unbelief are twin brothers, but so are righteousness and faith—and you get to choose every day which brothers you're running with in life. Your choice affects not only deep spiritual things like salvation, but everyday practical things like success at work or success at living at peace with others that day. Righteousness is both a spiritual concept and a practical way of living.

For instance, choosing between unbelief or belief in God's Word can affect something as tangible as buying a house—will you just accept that you'll have to pay that mortgage for thirty years or will you believe God's Word that your seeds will produce harvests, that you have favor with God and man, and that everything you touch prospers? Do you believe that one day you'll be able to live debt free . . . and do you believe it when you don't have enough cash for what you want? Ahhhh, faith starts wherever you are and lifts you up. Unbelief tears you down and sticks you below even the status quo! Faith lifts you up and shows you a future that is not just surviving but living in abundance—wherever you point your faith, that's where you are going to rise.

You rise first in your mind, and as you rise in your mind, you begin rising in your emotions, in your will, and in your passion in life. Unbelief or doubt railroads your morale. Faith and righteousness (doing what's right) causes you to soar with the eagles inside your own soul. The Most High God is called that for a reason— He is high and lifted up, and when you stick with Him and believe Him, you begin to go higher and are lifted up, too.

It's a win-win with faith and righteousness. It's a lose-lose with doubt and sin. I often say that sin will take you further than you want to go, keep you longer than you want to stay, and charge you more than you want to pay. Sin starts small, but in the end it'll take everything you've got. The antidote to sin is repentance—a quality choice to say "no" to what you've been missing the mark over. Doubt is serious business, and there is actually a connection to sin in doubt according to the Bible.

In a previous chapter, I told you a very hard scripture in Romans 14:23 that says, ". . . *whatsoever is not of faith is sin.*" Now, that's hard to hear! But I like the hard saying of this because it makes it much easier for me to avoid the temptation of doubting God Almighty! I don't want to sin against my God. I don't want to be so prideful as to think I know something He doesn't! I don't want to be a son who calls his Father a liar. My goal is to be a strong son, a son who lives with childlike faith and wonder, and has the guts to do what's right—even if it's hard.

People Who Get Out of the Ditches of Life— They Decided to Stop Thinking and Acting Like a Ditch-Dweller

I like scriptures like Romans 13:8 that tell me to owe no man anything but to love him. I know it's hard, but it's the goal for me to do that. Now, you can be broke and owe nobody anything. There are a lot of people on the street who have no debts, but they are not experiencing life and life in abundance like Jesus came to give. So, being debt free God's way, for me, is about having enough not to have to borrow, too. I want to be at a state like Deuteronomy

15:6 talks about, where I am so blessed that I can be a lender and not a borrower.

Now, if you aren't there, don't get under condemnation—I wasn't there for a long time either! But was that a goal of mine? Yes. Did I have faith that God could bless me and give me favor enough to bring me to that place in life? Yes. The point is that you start where you are in everything, whether it's spiritual, physical, or financial. For instance, if you need a mortgage to buy a house, you don't live in unbelief thinking God will never help you and you'll have to pay the note for thirty years. No, you choose faith and righteousness in the process and believe that you will not have to pay it for thirty years. You believe that you will have favor, unexpected blessings, and opportunities for prosperity. You believe that God will guide you to wisdom in practical ways to pay it off early, just as you believe that He will bring supernatural harvests of blessing on the seeds you sow into His kingdom work.

Now, if you tell someone who has no faith that you are believing to be debt free and they know your finances would make being debt free impossible, just realize that they are going by what they see—but you are determined to go by what you believe. That's the difference between a doubter and one who believes.

Remember that people like the status quo. It makes them feel good to know that everybody's in a ditch if they are in a ditch! But if you want out of that ditch, you'll have to think and do something the ditch-dwellers aren't thinking and doing. You can't act and think like a ditch-dweller if you want to get out. You'll have to cut a path for yourself with faith and righteousness that seems uncomfortable at first, and maybe even unbelievable to the ears of those walking in the ditch.

You have to decide that you don't want to live that way anymore. After all, you can do better. You've been born again—the limits are off because you serve a limitless God. He can do the impossible in your life like He did the impossible in mine. You have to decide that you are choosing faith over doubt no matter what. You're choosing to go back in time, so to speak, and live with childlike faith and wonder in Your Father—regardless of how you started out in life or what misery tried to teach you something apart from the truth.

Evil may be alive and well on the earth, but it is not alive and well in you.

You've chosen to do whatever it takes to follow His righteous Word, which means doing the practical "right" things that make you a good steward of your mind, your health, your relationships, and your finances, too. You've decided that you *know* God is with you; you know in Whom you have believed. You know that God is on your side, and your faith will bring you exactly what your heart desires—but only if you don't mentally bend to the debt-loving pressure of a world that would put a mortgage on your underwear if you let them! All they have are traps, but God is the key to getting out of every one of them. Put Him first and think well of yourself to yourself—don't let the enemy throw doubt in your mind about who you are.

Remember, you can hang with the doubt and sin brothers if you want to. Or you can hang with the faith and righteousness brothers and go higher in life. I'm reminded of The Righteous Brothers. Remember them? They sang that old song, Unchained Melody. I loved that song back in the day! "Oooooohhh my love, my darling, I've hungered for your touch" was the lyric, but you've got to change that to, "Oh my Lord, my God, I'm hungering for Your touch"—because all it takes is God's hand on your life to change everything around in you and for you.

Never forget! There are two sets of twins, and you get to choose who you live life with—I hope you choose those faith and righteousness brothers! They are the better choice for your life no matter where you come from, because they are going to bring you where you want to be. Go back in time and recapture the faith you were born with!

17

Learning to Be True and Faithful

YOU CAN'T CHANGE ANYTHING
UNTIL YOU'RE WILLING TO CHANGE *YOU*

I've been on the board of many churches and ministries. I remember one in particular whose board I decided to leave—and the reason was pretty simple. They didn't care about paying their bills. If they were short on money, they ran from those they owed. They hid. They would rather have done anything than face the people they owed.

I have a hard time believing people who claim true and faithful belief when they have poor and unfaithful conduct in the everyday affairs of life. Jesus told us to let our yes be yes and our no be no—in other words, stick to what you believe, say it, and don't live wishy-washy.

Many believers claim to have a true and faithful belief when it comes to the things of God, but you know it's just lip service because they aren't people of their own word. Some of these believers are in leadership. There's no shortage of people who preach one thing and do another. Our Christianity shouldn't be just words—though our words are important. Faith without works is dead, and that means we have to do right. If God is a keeper of His Word, then we should be keepers of our word, too.

Even if it hurts to follow through with what we said, we do our best to follow through—because that's what swearing to our own hurt in Psalm 15 means. Life isn't perfect. Things happen. Sometimes what we meant to do is no longer doable for one reason or another. If that's the case, it's our job to go to those involved and explain our situation and work out a plan with them. That's the right thing to do.

When I was on that board, I felt like following-through was irrelevant to the leaders of that church. I couldn't be a part of it anymore—because people shouldn't have to chase a church down to find out why they aren't fulfilling their commitments. Even if it's embarrassing, as believers (leadership especially) we have to do the right thing, and being upfront is the right thing to do.

True Belief Produces the Principles of True Conduct— I Make Every Single Effort to Do What I Say

When I tell my staff I'm going to give them time off for Christmas, they don't doubt that I'm going to give them time off for Christmas! If I tell them I'm going to give them a raise, they don't doubt that they'll see a raise on their next check. Why don't they doubt? They don't doubt because I have a pattern of good conduct when it comes to doing what I say.

In fact, if I say, "Everybody is getting a raise" in a staff meeting, they all cheer. Why? They cheer because they believe me, even though they don't have one extra dime yet. Think about that. I've never seen one person I told I'd do something for say, "Awwww, no, that isn't going to happen." Why? I have a history of good conduct.

Why do I believe Jesus? I believe Jesus because He has a history of good conduct. The Word is written evidence that He is not only great in belief but great in conduct. Jesus didn't walk around telling people one thing and doing another. As His disciples in this world, we shouldn't do that either.

I will never be the kind of man that people have to chase down to get what I promised them. My word is my bond. I like to say, "I want my word to be like God's!" which means if I tell you I'm going to do something, you can believe that I'm going to do everything I can to make sure I come through—even if it hurts! I think of it as part of my faith to have good character so that others can put faith in me, too. I want others to know that they can follow me as I follow Christ because I'm giving my best in this life (1 Corinthians 11:1). Much has been given to me, and so much is required from me—my goal is always to give my best and nothing less, and that's in my conduct as well as my offerings!

What keeps believers from keeping their word? Sometimes I think it's just plain old doubt—life situations arise and they doubt that they can fulfill what they said. They fall into worry. Some run and hide. They want to ignore their own promises just as much as they want to ignore the ones they made the promise to in the first place! If this is a struggle for you, let me help you out—you must never learn to doubt!

Ask for God's help and have faith that He is going to help you—don't doubt His ability to help you, and don't doubt your own character either. If it's a weak spot, let the weak say I am strong! Start saying that about yourself, "I've got a true and faithful belief in God and myself. I've got a true and faithful character, and my actions match my words!" Just say it. Even if it feels odd, just start reminding yourself of Who you serve. God keeps His Word, and you will keep yours, too.

Decide today that you're going to be known for keeping your promises. If things don't go as planned, decide that you're going to be humble enough to go directly to that person and tell them the situation—that you're going to make every effort to be open, honest, and ask for their mercy while you make things right. You'd be shocked at how merciful people can be when you're just flat honest and not trying to hide from them or con them in any way, shape, or form. Nobody likes a Christian con artist!

Before you ever break a promise to someone, realize that you first break it to yourself—and that damages your opinion of yourself in your own mind. Whether you realize it or not, it eats at you. Don't let it eat at you! All you have to do is ask for forgiveness from whomever you broke your word to, and then tell them you're sorry too—then start fresh. Let the blood of Jesus wash that guilt or shame away from you.

As a believer, you have to learn how to thrive. It doesn't just happen. Sometimes, when you're raised just to survive, you just don't know any other way to act than the wrong way.

I Was Violent Because I Saw Violence, but God Helped Me to Unlearn That Survival Mechanism

I did things the wrong way as a kid so much that the adults were worried about me. Now, I had my word—that meant something to me. I was the kind of kid who, if I told you I was going to hit you upside the head, I was going to hit you upside the head! I had a problem with violence.

If somebody told me, "You're too small to do anything!" my response wasn't, "Yeah, you're right." No indeed! My response was, "I may be small but a baseball bat isn't!" I came from a generation where it was normal to fight—and nobody called the cops. There weren't as many guns, but there sure were a lot of fists flying.

I was twelve years old when I put a bus driver in the hospital for three months by hitting him with a bat. He had wronged my sister, and it was payback time to me. They sent me to a psychiatrist because they thought it was so unusual, but they just didn't know how I'd been raised. Why was I that way? I was violent because I saw violence, and I experienced violence. I was beaten just about every single day. I couldn't get away from it. Nothing I did was right, and I was always being treated harshly. Guess what happens to some kids who grow up like that? They are hair-triggered to see wrongs coming. They are hair-triggered to react with a bigger stroke of violence than they see coming their way.

In other words, kids that experience violence at the hands of people they think should protect them are taught through the experiences that people aren't always on their side, even if they love them or like them. They have a nagging feeling that nobody really has their best interest at heart, and that it's a dog-eat-dog world where only the "strong" survive. Today, many people think strength lies in violence. Jesus did not teach that. The world teaches us that!

When everything and everybody feels like a possible threat, you know you are living in survival mode. Sometimes surviving looks like hiding. Sometimes surviving looks like addiction. Sometimes surviving looks like taking a bat to school when you think your voice alone is too small to be heard. But God changed me once I found Him, and He is the One Who helped me to unlearn that survival mechanism of violence. I don't know where I'd be today if I hadn't found God, but I know I'd be dead!

What the Devil Meant to Destroy Me, God Turned Around for Good in Me

Am I proud of the violence of my youth? Absolutely not. But I can look back now and see how I got there—I can see what lying to a child does, what hitting a child too hard and too often does, and I can see how easy it is to rob a child of the feeling of being heard or being safe. It's easy to turn a child into someone brokenhearted or someone who acts out in violence to themselves and others. Any idiot can do that.

As believers, though, it doesn't matter what was done to us, because the principles of true belief go beyond just rescuing us from our past—they create a new future for us as they heal our mind, shift our will, and sooth our emotions. God is a Healer of souls. He didn't just help me to survive; He turned it around completely and helped me to start thriving in life. Thriving is what Jesus was talking about in John 10:10 when He said, *"I am come that they might have life, and that they might have it more abundantly."* Survival and abundance are at opposite ends of the lifestyle spectrum. One is barely getting by mentally, physically, or financially. The other is overflowing with life's goodness in all those areas.

Man, what the devil meant to destroy me, God turned around for good in me. I know He will do the same for you. Maybe He already has! He'll do it for anybody. Sometimes we are so hurt by our past that we slide into offense. That's not good. I often say the difference between hurt and offense is that when you are hurt, you look for someone to heal you. But when you are offended, you look for someone to hurt. We release our offences against those who wronged us because we know the destruction of our heart and mind must end.

You see, doubting God can sometimes be merged in our minds with doubting people. We start to judge Him by them! But to succeed God's way, we need to take people out of our assessment of God. For instance, you may have been raised by Christians who didn't do the right things. People in a church somewhere, who led you to believe that it was all a farce, may have hurt you. Never judge Christ by the conduct of Christians—He's not them!

We are all human, and some people make a near art form out of living the opposite of what they say. Don't let that deter you from thriving as a believer. People are people, and not everybody's going the right way. That doesn't mean you have to go the wrong way, too. That doesn't mean you have to sacrifice a good and loving life just because you encountered some bad and hate-filled people.

The bad are mixed with the good in all areas of life, and until Jesus comes to separate the wheat from the chaff, that's just going to be the reality of life—and that includes church life, too. I know it's not right, but it is reality. Still, don't let a couple of idiots steal your faith and fill you with doubt about God. Again, He's not *them!*

You can't love God fully or believe His Word fully if you don't trust Him—and you will undermine your own ability to trust if you mistakenly judge God by the conduct of people. Most people who do that end up living with bitterness in one way or another. They both give up on God and turn to attacking those who still believe, or they end up going through the motions but not really believing God. They can't give it all they've got because they don't trust God. Until we let God off the hook for what people do, we can't live freely. We end up shackled with doubt and sometimes even glorifying it to others.

Freedom is a powerful thing that faith promotes from the soul level outward. It requires that we both let go and believe and that we sometimes fight for what we believe. "Fight the good fight of faith" is not about fighting against faith—it's about fighting for faith, and sometimes that is in our own mind. If we want to thrive, we have to put down the habit of being content to survive.

You Can't Change Anything Until You Are Willing to Change First

I never learned to doubt because once I let Jesus come into my life, I really let Him come into my life! I didn't hold back. I figured that if I served the devil with gusto before I got born again, I was going to serve Christ with gusto after I got born again. I was going to take Him at His Word. I was going to believe and give my new faith everything I had to give.

For me, nothing mattered but the new life I was forging with God in my heart. The weights of the world I had on my heart were released to God—and I didn't go back to pick them up again, even when life got tough. You see, I'd already seen how tough life can get, so it was no surprise. I knew that serving God didn't change the whole world; it changed me . . . and then it was my job to take His Word and change the situations of my life. In doing that, I could affect my family. In doing that, I could affect my friends. In doing that, I could affect my community and beyond.

You see, you can't change the world if you're not willing to let God change you first. You can't change anything in your life until you're willing to change first—you must go first on the inside, then you can focus on the outside. I like how Jesus says don't go picking at splinters in the eye of another before you take that log of wood out of your own eye first! Do what you have to do to see clearly. Then, go and help somebody else to see clearly, too. That's my paraphrase, but you get the point! You go first.

Too many believers today are so worried about the splinters in everyone else. They are so worried about the problems in the world and yet they don't deal with the problems in their own heart, much less their own house. We don't change the world from the outside in—we change it from the inside out.

So, if God loved people, then we can start loving people. If He didn't go back on His Word, then we don't go back on our word. If He said it's impossible to please Him without faith, then we choose to have faith! We change the world by starting with ourselves. We start from a place of belief, a belief that all things are possible for those who believe . . . because they *are*.

18

Spiritual Progress Is Attained by Strong Belief

CHURCH ISN'T ABOUT JUST WHAT YOU GET OUT OF IT

When I got saved, I began to get into the Word of God, and I didn't realize it then, but I was filling up the cracks and crevices of my mind with faith. Instead of sitting around debating this or that, I was just absorbing so much scripture that I didn't take time to doubt it. The Word started jumping off the page, so to speak. I couldn't get enough of what God had to say. So, whenever I could, I made sure I was in church to hear more.

Church is something some believers consider optional—but not me, and it's not because I'm a preacher now. Long ago, when I came to know Jesus, I made churchgoing a habit. I consider even just the act of going to be a part of leading a disciplined life, and I believe in having a disciplined life. Sometimes you have to tell your flesh "no" in one area so you can enjoy the benefits of "yes" in another area. As kids, we went to school not just to learn, but also to socialize with our peers. At church, your "peers" are your spiritual brothers and sisters—and so, what you learn is one part of going to church, but who you interact with is the other part.

Back when I got born again, I decided that I wouldn't put anything ahead of God. Sometimes, there were other things I wanted to do more than go to church, but I stuck to my decision that God would come first. I love sports, and sometimes I wanted to watch that on Sunday more than go to church—but I had enough sense to realize that sports couldn't help me the way hearing the Word could help me. I might have been a fan of a team, but I'd chosen to be a greater fan of the faith I gained by hearing the Word of God. There's nothing wrong with sports or hobbies, etc., but I decided that no matter what I loved in the natural, I would put God first—and doing that helped me in so many ways.

Matthew 6:31-34 says, *"Therefore take no thought, saying, What shall we eat? or, What shall we drink? or, Wherewithal shall we be clothed? (For after all these things do the Gentiles seek:) for your heavenly Father knoweth that ye have need of all these things. But seek ye first the kingdom of God, and His righteousness; and all these things shall be added unto you. Take therefore no thought for the morrow: for the morrow shall take thought for the things of itself. Sufficient unto the day is the evil thereof."* Now, I didn't have any physical needs when I got born again. I was successful and could buy whatever I wanted to eat, drink, or wear. But from that passage, I understood the principle of seeking God first. I could seek whatever else I enjoyed doing second, third, or fourth, but God had to be first.

I Could Preach Virtually Every Day, but I Want to Connect in Person at Church, Too!

Church isn't just about what you get out of it; it's about what you give God by putting Him first. I believe the discipline of putting God first is a principle that shows honor to God—it's a form of love and humility that says, "God, I love you so much, I want to put you ahead of everything else I enjoy. I recognize that You are God, and I honor You by going to church today." It's a practical form of honor to the Lord.

This is one thing we do as believers that sets us apart—we uphold the tradition of getting together as a congregation because we know there is *great* power in our unity. We don't just connect socially, we connect spiritually when the anointing falls and every person believing in the room becomes a conduit of God's presence. It's powerful, and I love it.

Hebrews 10:23-25 puts it this way: *"Let us hold fast the profession of our faith without wavering; (for He is faithful that promised;)*

And let us consider one another to provoke unto love and to good works: Not forsaking the assembling of ourselves together, as the manner of some is; but exhorting one another: and so much the more, as ye see the day approaching."

We help each other out just by being there because we naturally stimulate each other to be more loving and to do good things. When we connect with others and talk, we can become an encouragement to one another. At our church, we consider each other family, and our purpose is to lift one another up. When we all come together in praise to God, I've seen His anointing fall on all of us so strongly that people had a hard time standing up.

With all the technology we have today, there are many believers who don't see the importance of attending an actual church—but not me, and, again, it's not just because I'm a preacher. I could preach every day online or on TV, but I want to preach in church, too. I want to be in church with others. During the COVID-19 quarantine of 2020, that was one of the hardest things to give up. My wife and I found ourselves reaching out more on social media to preach and to interact, and we couldn't wait to get together again in person with our church family.

Now, the Word of God was the same at home as in the church, but there is something different about *"not forsaking the assembling of ourselves together"* in one building—God Himself knows that we need each other. We are social beings. We require connection to others. Some are more social than others, but none of us does well when isolated from other human beings. As people of faith, it's important that we see our community for what it is: a help during the strains and stresses of life.

When I'm Speaking, I Protect My Mind—
It's a Personal Conviction of Honoring God

One of the ways I combat doubt is to keep my mind clear before I'm scheduled to speak. A lot of my minister friends don't have a problem with going to the movies if there is a long break between services—but I can't do it. I choose not to do it, even though I love movies. I have no problem with movies whatsoever. But I am protective of my mind before a service. I just personally want my mind stayed on Christ. I always think, *Maybe God would want to speak to me about tonight's service. I don't want to be so absorbed in the movie that I miss what He would have me do tonight.*

Now, that's just me. It's a personal conviction of mine, and I am not telling you what to do. What I am saying is, I choose my state of mind. I feel that I must do that because I never know who is coming to a meeting. Maybe someone comes with stage four cancer and needs prayer. I don't want to lay my hands on someone and hear my brain start quoting lines about the dark side of the Force! I like the Star Wars franchise as much as the next person, but it doesn't belong in the prayer line! That's a joke, but you understand what I'm saying, right?

Spiritual progress can only be obtained by strong belief—and to keep my belief strong, I keep Him first and watch movies on days when I don't have to go and preach. But after? The next day? Oh, I can smell the buttered popcorn in my mind as I make my way to the theater! Have you ever been full from dinner and still ordered a large bucket of popcorn at the movies? If so, you are not alone. I love that stuff. I can eat so much of it that I can barely swallow another bite, but I still seem to take that one more bite.

God gives us richly all things to enjoy in this life—and there is nothing wrong with enjoying entertainment. Just remember that to progress spiritually, you must put the Spirit first. Honor God and God will honor you. It's that simple.

The Closer We Get to God in True Faith, the More We Experience His Radiating Goodness

We must have something to believe in and look forward to. It's the way humanity has been created to function. We're not created to live stagnant; we're created to grow. We're created to help one another to advance as well, and to build each other up. We make no good strides on this planet by doing the opposite! Everything Jesus did helped people. Heaven's description in the Word gives us an idea about not only the abundance and beauty of Heaven, but also the sheer goodness that exists the closer you get to God. The truth is that the closer we get to God in true faith, the more we experience His radiating goodness.

Church is a place where we can be prayed on by others of like precious faith. We go *with* our faith, though—we don't go just searching for other people's faith. It's a joint effort! So, let's talk about this a little bit. If we are sick and we read that by the stripes laid on Jesus' back we "are healed," then if we are believers, we must align our mind and heart with that truth. We must draw close to Him to feel the radiation of that good truth.

"Am sick" must be *less than* "are healed" in our own mind and heart, so to speak. We build our faith with the Word. And we must speak the Word over ourselves, too. We don't just repeat it like magic words. We let His Word seep into us until it's such a solid belief in our mind that we see it for what it really is: TRUTH.

We can even visualize the Words we read. We can "see" Jesus taking those beatings—with every hit with that hooked whip that tore the skin and muscles of His back, a disease was being paid for, a sickness was being paid for, or a condition of the body was being paid for. With His shed blood, you were gaining access to healing. Think of it that way. Make it personal. We must see that what He *did* overrides what our bodies are *doing*. It must be strong in our heart and mind because faith is believing.

I like to say that I was healed before I ever got sick. I like to pray scriptures of health and wholeness over myself, even though I'm not sick. I don't look at it like a prescription for health; I look at it as a maintenance plan! We access healing just like we access everything else from God: by faith, which is belief.

Even the unbeliever can have a good result with sheer thoughts. It's called the placebo effect! Why does it work? It works because God created us all to live by faith and not just sight. We were born believers! As Christians, we take that up even higher because our faith isn't only in ourselves or another human, but it is in the One Who made our mortal bodies.

So our faith has teeth, so to speak! It is stronger because it is in God Almighty—and it's even stronger when we come together in the unity of the faith and pray for one another in church. The corporate effect of letting go of everything and praising God together as a body is wonderful! I can honestly agree with David and say, *"I was glad when they said unto me, Let us go into the house of the Lord"* (Psalm 122:1) . . . now, I can't agree with him *every* single time, but I can most of the time!

I Will Preach Faith and Live by Faith Until I Cross Over into Heaven

They say that people who attend church live longer—if that's the case, I'm going to live a good long while! I don't even skip it when I go on vacation! Taking care of my spirit is something that I enjoy. I also try to take care of my flesh and blood body—I want to be around to see my granddaughter raise her children.

So, I eat well. I exercise. You see, I was born chunky. I've always fought my weight—so I know that if I let myself go, I could become as big as a house. I preach the good Word of God and it energizes not only my spirit, but also my body. I live my life giving and God blesses me in return, and I know that keeps my heart feeling good, too.

God has blessed me more than I ever imagined I'd be blessed—and my gratitude to Him for it is something that I know keeps me well, too. I'm grateful for my wife, Cathy. We've been married since 1970. She's my partner in everything, and I know God put her in my life and put me in her life for a purpose. We work together. I have an only child, who also has an only child, and we are all very close. In other words, I have a lot in my life to be happy about.

While some people do, I don't live for pleasure—I am motivated by purpose. Pleasure is a byproduct, but it's not what motivates me. That is my nature, I guess, and it suits my calling. I am a worker by nature. I always have been that way. I never wake up with "nothing to do," and to be honest, although I wouldn't mind trying that out for a little while, I think it'd drive me crazy to live like that for very long. So, considering all that, it always fascinates me when people ask me questions about my own death! And by the way they ask it, I can tell I'm more "alive" than they are, which is kind of funny to me.

People get worried, and with a very concerned voice, they ask me things like, "Brother Jesse, what if you get sick and die? What then?" I tell them that I will never deny a problem in my life, but I will deny its right to remain. If I get sick, I may hurt and I won't deny that, but I will still say, "by His stripes I am healed." Just like I wrote about priorities to teach you, I live this stuff! "I am sick" has to bow to "I am healed" in my heart and mind.

They aren't satisfied with that kind of answer, though. What they really want to know is what if something is missed, and what if by some reason I don't get healed . . . they want to know if faith is negated if we "die in faith." So, here's my take on that. If something were to happen to my body, and I believed God for my healing but I didn't receive healing in this life, guess what? I'd die in faith! So what!

Many have died in faith and I don't think of them as failing, so I wouldn't see myself as failing either. In fact, I'd venture to say that if I died due to sickness, it's probably because I chose to go—once you get close to the other side, it's hard to want to stay here in this sin-sick world. In fact, I think a lot more people than you'd ever imagine make that choice and never tell a soul!

Did you know that dying in faith has been done by many people in the Bible as well? Hebrew 11:13 says this before it gives a listing of names: *"These all died in faith, not having received the promises, but having seen them afar off, and were persuaded of them, and embraced them, and confessed that they were strangers and pilgrims on the earth."*

Some people just decide they want to go home. Some believers really get a vision of what it means to be a believer and where they actually come from. They know they are strangers and pilgrims on the earth. They know this body is just a temporary form and this life is just a temporary experience. We are eternal. So! Some say "NO!" even to healing because they see a better future off earth and want a better resurrection. Good Lord! I'm telling you, many have gone that way, and that's OK.

So, when people worry about me because I'm getting older, and when they ask about where my faith stands with sickness, I just tell them the truth, "Either we get healed here or we die and get healed there! The end result is the same—healed, whole, and doing good!"

There is no hatred or malice in Heaven. There's no poverty. There is no sickness or disease. None of the evils of this world are there, and none of what sin brought here is there either. Whatever is not of God is not in Heaven. Sometimes I think, *I want to go to Heaven, but I don't want to die.* I think many people are concerned about that! They think, *Will it hurt?* We all want to avoid pain and suffering, that is for certain.

As for me, if Jesus tarries and I go by way of the grave, I'm planning on having what I call a "good death." That means I'm going to Heaven with His joy in my heart, His peace in my mind, and His Word coming out of my mouth. This is what I'm believing God for in my life, should I pass before Jesus comes back. I want to go out of this world with the same purity that I came into this world with—in childlike faith and with pure, openhearted wonderment.

Until then, I'm determined that my true belief is going to dictate my conduct. I'm not going to live with that sickness called doubt. I refuse to live in sin and perpetuate the misery. I want to spread joy and the boldness of faith, and I want to tell everybody about my Jesus—I want them to know that if He can change a man like me, well, He can change anybody!

I'm living, walking, and talking proof that the love of God can change the heart of a man, and the Word of God can order His steps in a new and wonderful direction. Like 1 John 4:4 says, greater is He who is in *me* than he who is in this world! The devil can't keep me blind anymore; the light is way too bright. If God be for me, who can be against me? The devil can't convince me that anyone or anything is more powerful than my God.

God's Word is called the sword of the Spirit and I'm determined to live my life swinging that spiritual weapon—letting the living words of God come out of my mouth and into this earth in order that others might know the truth that can set them free. It's not God's will that any should perish in misery, doubt, or that soul-killing condition of sin, but that *all* should come to believe.

My life is dedicated to preaching because I *know* people are worth it. No matter the culture or the color, God wants us to love people because He loves people. He loves us enough to tell us the truth—not to placate us or lie to us, but to remind us that we can overcome the devil and all his works if we just have the guts enough to believe He's with us.

People aren't God's enemy. The only enemy is Satan and all the work he does to agitate, instigate, and perpetuate evil. We were *all* born with faith no matter how long God's enemy has been working to convince us otherwise—and that means we can all have the capacity to believe God and see results.

So, let doubt go and let faith rise, and live your life with one eye on Heaven! Just see what God has in store for you as you let your childlike faith shine. Remember that the problems of the world are many, but the solution to mankind's real problem—the heart condition that keeps him locked in low-level ways of acting towards himself and others—can only be solved by reuniting with the Father of us all. Jesus is the way to reconnecting to God. He's the Way, the Truth and the Life, and no man goes to the Father except by Him (John 14:6).

I don't know about you, but as the world's ways get more evil, I see that the righteous are getting more righteous—the polarization is no coincidence. Let's focus on the light of God and not get caught up in the darkness. Let's focus on the good life that comes from following His Word, and let's share the love of Jesus with others. We never know when He'll show up in the sky, and I don't know about you, but I want to take as many with me as possible.

I'm awaiting the return of Jesus more every day! But, hey, if Jesus doesn't come to get me, I'm going to Him! I'm going to Heaven either way. And if the world is still turning then, I pray *every* Word of God that I've preached finds the ears and hearts of the ones who not only need it but also have a passion to spread it. I pray that this torch of faith that was passed to me so many years ago is taken up by another who's ready to run!

Who knows? Maybe that's you . . . don't doubt it if so. This world needs all the help it can get!

19

Doubt Is an Identity Thief

IT HAS NO FACE, BUT IF YOU LET IT, IT *WILL* STEAL YOURS

Doubt makes you forget who you are in Christ. It's an identity thief. Doubt doesn't have a face, but if you indulge in it too much, it'll steal yours. Like a man who looks in the mirror and then walks away forgetting what he looks like, a man who only reads or hears the Word but doesn't actually *do* it will end up searching for his identity. I like to say that if you're a Christian but you can't recognize who you are or the things you're doing anymore, it's likely that doubting God has become your habit. It's an easy fix, but you really have to see what you're doing sometimes just to make the change to faith.

To doubt God is to mock God—it's that serious. It's like saying you know better when it comes to you than God does, even though He is God and He created you. What a joke! This means that doubting God is at odds with your growth. It makes you the enemy of your own self-discovery.

God's instruction is there not to just help us live better but to know ourselves better—God is a revealer. The more we learn from Him and fellowship with Him, the more we reveal our true character—the person we were created to be, you know, before the world got its hooks in and started tearing at us. The more comfortable we are with God, the more comfortable we'll be with ourselves because the closer we get to Him, the more He reveals the wonder of who we really are.

Where do you really get to know yourself? It's not just by sitting around reading the Bible—it's what you *do* after you read (hear) that helps you know yourself. This is about action. It's about what you go out and do.

James 1:1-25 is a great passage that warns us not to be a "hearer" who doesn't take action. If you let yourself slip into that, God's Word says that you'll forget who you really are—you'll have identity issues and lose the freedom that is in Christ. And, in that forgetting and losing, you'll bypass blessing, too. James 1:23-25 puts it this way: *"For if any be a hearer of the Word, and not a doer, he is like unto a man beholding his natural face in a glass: For he beholdeth himself, and goeth his way, and straightway forgetteth what manner of man he was. But whoso looketh into the perfect law of liberty, and continueth therein, he being not a forgetful hearer, but a doer of the work, this man shall be blessed in his deed."*

Notice the word "deed"—notice that your blessing is linked to what you do and not just what you say. Notice that the ability to recognize yourself (who you *really* are, the person God *created* you to be) fades the further you get away from action—from *doing* what you *hear* in God's Word. It's hard to *do* what you doubt! It's interesting that the Word links identity issues with being a hearer only, and that it equates freedom and blessing to actions and deeds.

Our Self-Knowledge Is Linked to God; Our Self-Discovery Is Born in the Heat of Action

You know, we all have that moment in our life when we wonder where we come from. Those issues are in the heart of every person because we were created to know our Father God—in Him we find our identity as His children, born of God, with an eternal destination that lies outside of this world.

We are in the world but not of the world. We are spirit first and foremost, again, having a temporary human experience. This desire to know who we are and where we come from can sort of be called a God-gene—our self-knowledge is forever linked to God, the One Who created us. Until we *"looketh into the perfect law of liberty, and continueth therein . . . being not a forgetful hearer, but a doer of the work,"* we can't really know ourselves well enough to satisfy that craving for inner peace.

Our self-discovery is something that is revealed as we move. It's born in the heat of action—in the day-to-day choice to be a doer of the Word, and not just a hearer who deceives himself. A hearer will talk about believing and not believe. A hearer will talk about loving and not love. A hearer can even preach all day long on Sunday and still be a miserable human being searching for who he or she really is in this world once he goes home. That's because identity is built from knowing who you are in Christ and *doing* what you're believing, praying, and saying!

So, where does faith begin? Faith begins at the thought level. It's a choice to believe *after* you hear. That choice is an action in and of itself. You are a doer in the mind before you are a doer in everyday life. That's why you should catch the doubt quickly in your own mind—because the longer you linger, the less you'll act. Doubt is an enemy of action, just as much as it is an enemy of faith. It's an identity-thieving face-stealer!

You will learn more about yourself in *doing* the Word than you will ever learn about yourself just thinking and talking about the Word. Faith without works is dead! It's worthless and not good for anything but the tickling of our ears. Life is moving forward all the time; your faith should be moving forward, too.

Have you ever met a "hearer only" kind of Christian? They say one thing and do another so much that you can set your watch to their hypocrisy because, man, it's coming at you every day! These are the thoroughly judgmental believers who never pass up an opportunity to cut somebody down. It's as if their heart knows they're in the wrong by not acting on the Word, but since they don't *want* to be wrong, they will push that away quickly and focus on scanning the world for *everybody else's* wrong! Hearers have forgotten who they are and Who they serve, just like James 1:23-25 says, and so they've lost their freedom in Jesus.

The Perfect Kind of Liberty, a Better Kind of Freedom

Freedom is a great thing. Most people equate being "free" in life with just being able to do whatever they want—that means being able to do whatever you want with no rules or interference—but that's not the kind of "freedom" God sees as liberty. For instance, think about an addict with all the money in the world to feed his addiction. He may be doing what he wants to do. He may have all the financial ability in the world to keep on doing what he wants to do. Is he free? No, he's a slave to an act or a substance. I know that's an extreme example, but I hope you understand the idea. Plenty of people do whatever they want to do and are still slaves to their own choices. They may have the world's kind of personal freedom and be able to do whatever they want, but they are still not free in their souls.

So, what is the "perfect law of liberty" that the scriptures talk about? It's talking about the Word of God. The perfect law of liberty is the freedom we find through salvation and the principles of God in His Word, which, if applied, give us freedom at a much deeper level. God's principles set you free as you hear them, don't doubt them, and do them. A lot of people read the Word and still live bound; that's because the truth can only set you free if you know it and act on it. Repeating words you don't get or never doing what you learn is "hearing only," and it doesn't make you free.

Liberty is something most want, even though some people fear their ability to handle it. Some would rather turn over the reigns of their own life just to avoid the responsibilities of freedom. But God knows that if we only knew Him and ourselves better, we'd realize there is nothing we can't handle with Him. We don't have to fear freedom. God believes in us. He believes in us more than we believe in ourselves! That's why His Word is so challenging. It gets to the root of our fears if we let it, and challenges us to have faith. We don't "work on ourselves" so much as we start to "reveal ourselves" to ourselves through Him!

The more we renew our mind to His Word and His ways, the more our will and emotions shift so that we can let go of fear and walk in the freedom we were born to have. Even the impossible is doable for us and the Lord knows it, which is why He said it. He just wants us to know it, too! Everybody wants to be blessed in some way, and God wants that for us, too. But it's hard to live blessed God's way unless you know who you are and Whose you are.

You're God's family. You learn who you are by being in the presence of the Father Who made you in the first place! You learn who you are not just by hearing Him but acting upon what He's said is right and good. Day by day, as you practice doing things His way, you learn about yourself—where your weak spots are and where you're strong already. When things go "wrong," well, that's when you see what you're made of.

To be "blessed in deed" like James 1:25 says, you have to do something with what you hear. If God says to love, then you've got to love even the unlovable. You can't speak love and act in hatred and expect to be blessed in deed. If God says to give and you don't, then you can't expect to be blessed in deed.

Your deeds are blessed when they are in line with what God said—and the more you act on the Word, the more freedom you'll feel as God's child. It has a compound effect. The more you act, the more you know yourself. It's as if you prove to yourself over and over Whose you are, and in that proving, you gain greater confidence.

One day, you will look back and see that what was once a weak spot for you is now a testimony of God's power in your life. Suddenly, you have a story to tell and you can tell it from a place of confidence. You've been there and done that. You know who you are in Christ, and the story you tell? Well, it's one that no "hearer only" can tell. It's a story with action and one that people can relate to . . . and that makes *you* a bold light in the darkness and a vision of hope for somebody living just like you once did.

God Already Made You—Stop Letting the World Mold You

The world is full of pushers. They want you to talk a certain way, look a certain way, act a certain way, and find your place in their warped system—there's always somebody trying to tell you how to be you! What are they doing? They are trying to get you to fit into a mold that God never made you to fit into. In trying to get you to conform to the ways of an ungodly world, they are attempting to give you an identity outside of who you already are in Christ.

When people are constantly trying to sell you things or tell you things in life that they promise will make you "better" in some way, you have to ask yourself why. You aren't broken if you have Jesus because He's not broken, and He lives in you. You don't need fixing no matter how much they tell you that you do. All you need is for the real you to be *revealed* . . . and the first person you need to be revealed to is *you*!

The most important thing you can remember in this is that God already made you and He loves who He made! Stop letting the world mold you and recognize the good thing God did when He made you. Stop listening to the lies that are always telling you that you aren't good enough. The pure state of who you are in Christ is wonderful—and that's what you reveal every time you accept God's Word over the world's opinions.

None of us are perfect, including you, but Satan has no new tricks. He's been cutting down human beings since the beginning. Even in tempting Eve, he was essentially telling her that she wasn't enough—that God made some kind of mistake and she needed to disobey God in order to be more whole. What a bunch of junk! Satan is a self-esteem killer first before he's anything else. Anything that tries to steal, kill, or destroy your opinion of who you are in Christ is not good and not from God. God is the lifter of your head, not the stomper of your heart!

So you are not perfect, so what? Christ *is* perfect, and He lives in you—Christ in you, the hope of glory (Colossians 1:27). So you have hope! When you mess up and step outside of your Christlike true nature, recognize it and ask for forgiveness, shake off the dust, and then keep on walking. Step by step, God will help you to become who He meant you to be—but you'll never see your best self revealed by chasing or conforming to the world's opinions of who you are. In Christ is where your true identity lies.

People can criticize you all they want. They can try and pick out your flaws and call you something you're not. Don't let anybody guilt you into being what you are not—you aren't the world's child; you are God's child. In Christ, you are pure as snow. You are redeemed. That's the beauty of salvation. Jesus' blood washes all the "missing the mark" (sin) away. Every day, your aim should be to walk in the truth and purity that you know.

We are all living our lives one day at a time, and every day I hope you learn more, hear more, and then go out and do more that is in line with the good that you know. As you focus on Jesus and on the Words of life, they renew your mind so that you can act on them and create a better day for yourself, your family, and the world beyond. The discipline of it is nothing compared to the outcome. The more you let the Word do its work in you, and the more you keep your heart soft and become a "doer," the more quickly your "revealing" will be—to yourself first, and then to everybody around you.

Never forget that the world will try to sell you all sorts of things to give you a new "face"—to foster an identity they're trying to sell you. Some will even try to warp the goodness within you, offering all sorts of deals and ideas to twist you into what they'd prefer you to be. Guess what? The best "you" that you'll ever be is the real, God-centered, perfect law of liberty you, regardless of what they say or what they're selling! You are free in Christ; don't let the world chain you with their confusion! Let the Christ in you rise up and remember this: God's truth cuts through human confusion like a hot knife cuts through butter! The Holy Spirit Who lives in you isn't confused. Don't be swayed by the liars in this world who just want to put down what God has already wonderfully made—you!

The Blessings in Deeds and the Hearer's Dilemma

The Word challenges us to get wisdom and get understanding. As we follow God's Word and allow it to reveal our true character in Christ, we reap the blessings of being who we really are—and, again, that affects us practically because, as we use wisdom and understanding, we become "blessed in deed" as James 1:25 says.

Blessings follow wisdom—and it's wisdom to believe. It's foolish to doubt God, and if you want to know more about the difference between the foolish and the wise, read Proverbs! The whole book is full of wisdom, but you really need Jesus and a close relationship with God to tap into that wisdom. It's one thing to read something; it's another thing to apply it!

I think one of the most confusing ways to live is to say one thing and do another—it's the "hearer's" dilemma. It's how the devil gets hypocrisy into the Church and into believers who don't believe. They talk the talk but don't walk the walk, and because they don't act, they don't see results. Acting on the Word helps *you* prove to yourself that it will work for you, which grows your confidence in yourself, too. That means every time you stretch your faith, you have past victories that you can rehearse to encourage yourself for the next victory.

Again, all of us are growing and learning, so nobody's perfect, but it's better to stretch your faith in God and be passionate than to pretend with the rest of the hearers and talkers. If a believer is willfully choosing to avoid God's truth, they are *not* going to be very blessed in their deed. God says He's not going to be mocked—whatever we sow, that's what we reap (Galatians 6:7). We can ask for mercy and grace. God can even save us from our own destruction. But if we want to live a good and more blessed life in general, it is always going to be in our best interest to just plain *do* what we know to do!

It's so important to believe God and to believe in your own worth and value to Him. You have everything it takes to be the child God created, so never doubt your own worth. Doing that is like calling God a liar—and He thought you were worthy of His Son's sacrifice. He believes in you, so believe in Him enough to believe in *you*, too! Just accept that God is always truthful. Don't doubt that.

Remember, a man who believes God to be untruthful will be untruthful himself—in fact, the first person he'll lie to is himself!

Satan Is a Serial Killer, and His Target Was Innocence from the Beginning

Adam and Eve mocked God in action, and they ended up walking out of paradise naked, afraid, and confused about where to go next. Again, what did the serpent use to tempt Eve? He tried to tell her that she was lacking as a human being by not having the knowledge of both good and evil. What a joke. Is innocence worth robbing? Only to the devil and those who follow his ways!

Do we think babies are *lacking* because they don't know evil yet? Do we look at an innocent child and criticize them for their innocence? Do we deliberately go out of our way to make sure they know evil early? Again, only if we are following the devil! A person who understands the value of God's goodness knows that innocence is worth protecting. Most of us, after getting a good look at the evils of this world, wish we could go back in time and be that innocent again! Not the devil, though. He is a serial killer, and his target was innocence from the very beginning.

Adam and Eve weren't "lacking," but they were being lied to. You see, we may not always like God's instruction, but it doesn't make it any less good for us. Eve didn't like being told to leave the fruit alone in the first place, but it was good for her to leave it alone. God was protecting her innocence while Satan was trying to steal it—and it's interesting to note that he didn't approach Adam first. Women always seem to get a rawer deal when it comes to being criticized for who they are, and that started back then with the devil, too! If you are a woman, don't fall for that junk! God loves you, God made you, and you aren't lacking as a human being.

In fact, don't let the devil lie to you about lacking anything by being saved and following God's ways either. The world has nothing to offer you in comparison to living in Christ. In Christ, you have everything you need to live that pertains to life and godliness. In His Word, you have principles and guidance that will lead you to prosper spiritually, physically, financially, and in any other way that you choose to focus upon. God is not just enough for you; He's more than enough for you, and He lives and moves and has His being in *you* (Acts 17:28). So, when "they" criticize you, they are criticizing the God in you just as much!

When You Know Who You Are, You Won't Chase the Praise of People

I've made up my mind that whether the people praise me or hate me, I'm going to live the way God has shown me in His Word. I have been "delivered from the people," as Acts 26:17 says! Some people like me; some hate me. Now, it feels better to be liked than hated, that is for sure! But does it change who I am? Does it change my opinion of myself? No indeed. If I thought like that, I'd be living on an emotional rollercoaster, and I'm not. It's Christ Who gives me this insulation against the lack mentality of chasing the praise of others—I've just read too much Word and experienced too much of His love for anybody to change my opinion of myself as God's child. Besides, people are fickle!

Jesus Himself knew firsthand how fickle the people can be. One day they were filling the streets praising Jesus and waving palms as He entered a city crying, "Hosanna!" One week later, they were filling the streets yelling, "Crucify Him!" That alone should show you how unreliable the opinions of people can be. If they turned on Jesus, they'll turn on you, too, if you're standing for something good. I've found that as quickly as a crowd will praise you, they'll turn and cut you, too. So, why give them the power over your heart? If God is your guide, then your opinion of yourself shouldn't change either way.

That's why I always take the praise and the criticisms of people with a grain of salt. I see too many good people who go astray by letting praise go to their head or criticism go to their heart. One puffs you up with pride; the other makes you not want to leave the house! The truth is that when you know who you are in Christ and that is your centerpoint for your opinion of yourself, you don't feel the need to chase the praise of people. There isn't enough praise in the world to fill up an empty heart.

If you find that you do that, just know this: you don't need anybody's approval—God already approves of you. *You* just need to approve of you, too! You are more than enough every day and twice on Sundays, as they say. The point is that twenty-four hours a day, you are more than enough. To be carnally minded leads to death, but to be spiritually minded leads to life and peace—and the carnal mind always looks to people and their opinions more than it looks to God and His Word (Romans 8:6).

Praise is not a measurement of intrinsic worth any more than criticism is a measurement for it. People are worth so much to God that He sent His only Son to die for the world, and His Word is full of encouragement to remind us how loved we are. Seeking approval from people to fill a lack in the heart is how many go astray. When you don't know who you are in Christ, you're at risk for mistaking all sorts of things for love. You'll take all kinds of substitutes just to feel worthy of love and admiration.

Plenty of famous and celebrated people get to the top of their fields and experience amazing accolades and still don't feel like they're enough inside. Plenty of people live trying to become what others want just to feel like they measure up.

If our opinions of ourselves are based on what others think, we'll always be jumping through hoops and changing in order to be accepted. In Christ, we find the love and acceptance we need at a soul level—it makes us realize we are *more* than enough in every way and that we have enough love inside for the world, too.

Always remember that nobody can praise you enough or ignore you enough to change the fact that you are loved by God. His love never ends. Refuse to doubt His love for you. Refuse to doubt yourself as you live in Christ. If praise comes, when you know who you are in Christ, just enjoy it—but never let it affect who you are or what you do. And after being praised, if the tide turns and you get criticized up a storm, just let it roll off your back. Let it be no big deal—just another day of never doubting that no matter what "they" say, *you* are God's beloved and He's made you a blessing going somewhere to bless and be blessed! When you start feeling that way, you'll know that you've been "delivered from the people" like I have. It's great!

Be confident in your role as a doer of the Word—the more you hear and do, the more you'll know yourself. You'll get to a point that *nobody* and *nothing* will be able to confuse you about *who* you are or *Whose* you are! Your identity will be grounded in the Lord, and you'll be "blessed in deed" as a result.

Push the Light and Keep Your Eyes on Jesus

IMPOSSIBLE THINGS HAPPEN WHEN THE WINDS ARE CONTRARY

Jesus lost His cousin, John the Baptist, to the vengeance of an angry woman named Herodias, who was sleeping with the King's brother. John said something about it and she got back at him by complaining to King Herod, who threw John in jail. Later, at a party, Herodias danced for Herod and he was so smitten that he asked her what she wanted in return. Herodias said she wanted John's head on a plate. So, at the spiteful woman's request, King Herod beheaded John the Baptist for her pleasure. It was nothing short of vengeance and a tragedy to Jesus, too.

John was the forerunner for Jesus. He wasn't just Jesus' cousin; he was also the one who Jesus submitted to for baptism. John was powerful, and Jesus loved him and admired his great boldness and faith. What did Jesus do after losing John the Baptist? You know He was hurting inside. He loved His cousin, and John's death was so senseless—done on a whim, like it was nothing. John was a great man cut down too early, and his death was a true loss.

How many people in this world have died senselessly? Maybe it's happened to you or someone you know—a death that never had to happen, a real criminal act perpetrated by a person who just didn't care. It would be human nature to feel the great tragedy and loss, and get enraged enough to go right back for the throat of the one who committed the crime. Nobody would slight you for wanting to do it either. We understand justice as human beings . . . but that is not what Jesus did. How did He react? Jesus responded to the malicious intent of dark minds by going out and pushing the light.

Jesus Reacted to Senseless Darkness by Pushing the Light— Healing, Preaching, and Providing in Response to Loss

When He heard about John, Jesus got in a ship and sailed to where the desert met the water—it seems like His first reaction was to be alone, something we all instinctively do when in pain. But people knew Jesus, and when they heard where He was going, they followed Him. Jesus didn't run away from them or cry to them or even talk about John. He immediately looked at the need right in front of Him, and there was plenty of it to see.

The Word says that Jesus saw the people around Him and was moved with compassion for them—even though John was still on His heart, Jesus reached out His hands to the people and began to pray for them to be healed. Think about it: Jesus healed *others* in response to His own loss. Jesus didn't let rage overtake Him (I want you to notice that); He moved in compassion through His own pain instead of rage.

After healing people, Jesus preached. And before you know it, His disciples came to Him with a people-problem—they told Jesus that they were too far out to buy food, and since it was time to eat and the people were getting hungry, Jesus should send them away so they could deal with their own hunger. Jesus looked at His disciples and said, and I'm paraphrasing, "They don't need to go anywhere. *You* give them something to eat" (see John 6).

You see, Jesus wasn't just about talking the talk—He was about action. He didn't want something like a hungry belly to get in the way of the people getting the spiritual food they needed, too. Jesus understands it all—if He was only interested in spiritual growth, He would have done exactly what the disciples said. He would have sent them away. He didn't, because He's not just interested in your spiritual growth—He's interested in you being full and entire wanting nothing, spiritually, physically, and financially. If it pertains to life and godliness, if it's something you need or desire, it fits into the realm of what Jesus wants to do for you.

Of course, the disciples didn't know what to do after Jesus told them to handle the problem of the hungry multitude. They started looking around, and sure enough, there was one little boy with a two-piece fish dinner. His mother had probably brought him to hear Jesus, and, apparently, he offered his lunch when the disciples looked around for a solution.

Two fishes. Five loaves. Jesus took that boy's seed, blessed it, broke it into pieces, and gave it to His *disciples* to hand out—notice that the miracle of feeding the five thousand that day did not happen in Jesus' hands. It happened in the hands of the disciples. The two fishes and five loaves multiplied as *they* handed it out.

As a believer, you have to be willing to take the little things from God first before you can see them multiply in your hand. You have to be a willing receiver and a willing giver, too. If you can't receive, you will not see the multiplication in your giving. It must flow to you, through you, and back to you again—this is the way God works. *"Give and it shall be given to you; good measure, pressed down, and shaken together, and running over, shall men give into your bosom"* is about the cycle of giving and receiving (Luke 6:38). The boy gave to Jesus what the disciples in turn gave to others after Jesus blessed it. Where was the doubt in all of this? It was nowhere to be found, which is why it all manifested so quickly.

Doubt wasn't in the mind of the disciples that day—if it had been, nothing could have been done. Remember, Jesus had been to His hometown at one time trying to help people, but nothing could be done, save a few healings, because nobody believed. Jesus needed His disciples to be on the same page that day, and thank God that they were, because we have the story to read today. It's a testimony of the disciples' refusal to doubt Jesus just as much as it was a testimony of the boy's generosity to give what he had, as well as Jesus' power to believe God would provide if He blessed and broke the bread into pieces. Notice He began with something small, and as long as they were giving it out, more was provided by God to give.

The Bible says they all ate and were full. They weren't just barely full with their stomachs still growling; they were so full that they had twelve baskets of leftovers. That's called "more than enough," and it's a hallmark of Jesus' touch on a situation when people have enough guts to stop doubting and just believe. He is a Master at turning the little things into "too much."

"Gather up the fragments that remain, that nothing be lost" (John 6:12) was Jesus' command when confronted with the "too much"—because although Jesus understood abundance, He wasn't a wasteful Man. He didn't waste the blessings of God. Who do you think got that overflow of bread and fish? I have a feeling that boy who sowed his meal got a whole lot of that harvest, maybe all of it. But one thing is for sure, the healings and the provision were done because nobody doubted, and they were done during a time when Jesus had just experienced personal loss.

There is something powerful about personal loss. You know really quickly where you are with God by how you react—not how you feel, but how you choose to react. It's where the rubber meets the road when it comes to believing God. Some lose all hope and let the anger of unjust situations make them just as unjust. However, Jesus is our example. When hurt, He immediately retreated to be alone and pray—but when He saw the people, He had compassion and used His hurt as a vehicle to meet their needs. Jesus reacted to His own hurt by choosing to be a Healer. Jesus reacted to His own hurt by choosing to be a Provider . . . a giver of "too much" in a time of "not enough."

Don't you think Jesus had a moment of wanting to call fire down from Heaven to burn up Herod and that evil woman who called for John's head to be served to her on a plate? You better know it! The Word tells us that He was tempted just like we are—and let me tell you, it's tempting to want to hurt those who hurt you. It's tempting to want to destroy when something you've had has been destroyed. But we don't serve a "tit for tat" and a "take that" kind of God—we serve One Who understands the power of pushing the light.

Today, we see so much desire for vengeance, for vindication, for payback—but as believers, we don't deal in darkness. We push the light.

Jesus Tries to Go Back to the Plan, but the Fourth Watch Awaits

What does Jesus do next after He heals, preaches, and feeds the five thousand? The meeting is over and He goes right back to His original plan—Jesus sends His disciples back to the ship and heads to the mountains to be alone and pray. Remember, He's hurting, He's just given out to all these people, and now He wants to be alone. He gains peace and strength through praying in nature. It's His habit to get alone with God in this way. I love nature. I like being in the mountains when it's cold.

You know, we could take a lesson from Jesus in the importance of getting out of the cities and the concrete jungle sometimes and just being in nature more. If Jesus did it so often, it has got to be a good thing to do! Let's read the actual scripture now, because I want you to see that Jesus isn't on that mountain for very long before He is needed again—but this time by Peter, the water-walking disciple.

> And straightway Jesus constrained His disciples to get into a ship, and to go before Him unto the other side, while He sent the multitudes away.
>
> And when He had sent the multitudes away, He went up into a mountain apart to pray: and when the evening was come, He was there alone.
>
> But the ship was now in the midst of the sea, tossed with waves: for the wind was contrary.
>
> And in the fourth watch of the night Jesus went unto them, walking on the sea.
>
> And when the disciples saw Him walking on the sea, they were troubled, saying, It is a spirit; and they cried out for fear.
>
> But straightway Jesus spake unto them, saying, Be of good cheer; it is I; be not afraid.
>
> And Peter answered Him and said, Lord, if it be Thou, bid me come unto Thee on the water.
>
> And He said, Come. And when Peter was come down out of the ship, he walked on the water, to go to Jesus.
>
> But when he saw the wind boisterous, he was afraid; and beginning to sink, he cried, saying, Lord, save me.
>
> And immediately Jesus stretched forth His hand, and caught him, and said unto him, O thou of little faith, wherefore didst thou doubt?
>
> And when they were come into the ship, the wind ceased.
>
> Then they that were in the ship came and worshipped Him, saying, Of a truth Thou art the Son of God.
>
> MATTHEW 14:22-33

The first watch is the first three hours of the trip. The second watch is the next three hours, and the third watch is the next—so by the time they are at "the fourth watch," the disciples have been up all night in the storm. It's the beginning of dawn now. This is when they see Jesus walking on the sea, and they were more troubled by that sight than the wind and waves that had been knocking them around for nine hours!

They cried out with fear. They didn't cry out with faith. Now, they'd just heard Jesus preach. They saw Him heal. They literally were the miracle hands that passed out the miracle fish and bread to over five thousand people. Yet, when they see Jesus, they cry out in fear. This shows you that human nature can't be convinced by eyes alone, because even if you believe God and see something wonderful, the moment you see something that is bigger than that? Well, your mind will react! It'll say, "No! This can't be!" even if you're looking at God. It's just the way the brain works—which is why you have to make a deliberate choice to suspend judgment and simply believe the Word.

The fourth watch is the last watch they'll make because they won't have to stay up wondering if they're going to die in the wind and the waves. Jesus shows up on the fourth watch. I believe that we are living in fourth watch times today. From Adam to Noah, the first watch. From Noah to Moses, the second watch. From Moses to Jesus on the earth, the third watch. From Jesus' time on the earth to Jesus' return in the sky, the fourth watch. Jesus is coming back!

The wind was contrary on the sea that day. The winds of change are contrary in the earth today. But impossible things happen when the winds are contrary! Look around. Right is considered wrong. Wrong is considered right. The stealing, killing, and destroying of people is global, and many are watching the wind and waves, wondering if we as the human race will make it out alive. Oh, we will make it out alive!

Jesus is coming back, and He's not coming when it's peaceful. He's coming just like He came on the sea that day long ago—when it is nothing but tumultuous, at a time when even believers who have seen His hand work miracles look around and can't see a way out. The winds of change are raging right now, and I'm praying that dawn is about to break soon, aren't you? I'm ready to see Jesus!

Doubt Subtracts Joy, Divides Attention, and Multiplies Fear, but the Spirit of Faith Is the Spirit of Adventure

When we put our eyes on Jesus and walk by faith, there is no failure. Even if we lose focus and our eyes go to the winds and waves for a moment, if we look to Him quickly like Peter did, Jesus will always be there reaching out to help us get back up on the water and start walking by faith again. The spirit of faith is a spirit of adventure.

It's fun doing what you once thought was impossible. Healing brings joy. Peace makes your heart feel light. Faith makes you think about what's possible with God on your side. Faith opens up your heart so that you start imagining the best instead of fearing the worst. On the other hand, doubt *never* creates good emotions.

Doubt multiplies fear—Peter began fearless, and that's why he stepped out of the boat. He wouldn't have taken one step onto the water if he'd doubted that it was possible. Looking at Jesus, though, Peter *knew* he could do it, and so he did. If anything *can* be done, experience and skill will do it; but if something *can't* be done, only faith can do it. Once you get that, it's easier to have faith. After all, if you know you can't do it on your own anyway, why not look to Jesus and believe Him? What do you have to lose? You have everything to gain and win!

The moment we begin to worry and doubt is the moment we start sinking, just like Peter. When we sink into fearful thoughts, we are predicting a future that we are making as we think the thoughts—we are calling those things that be not as though they were, but doing it in the negative sense.

If we sow doubt, we get more doubt. We perpetuate a problem in our mind first, and our life tends to follow the direction of our greatest belief. Remember Job's famous declaration, *"For the thing which I greatly feared is come upon me"*—and refuse to be like Job. Instead, think of what you want and have faith, saying, "The things I'm believing the most are coming upon me!"

Doubt divides attention—Peter wouldn't have ever begun to sink in the first place if he hadn't moved his eyes from Jesus to the waves hitting at his feet. Sometimes we tend to look around more than we look to God. This isn't good if we are trying to walk by faith and not sight. Impossible situations change all the time. There are so many testimonies of people who've been healed or gotten out of debt or went on to do something everybody thought was impossible. I once heard someone say that you should never take a "no" from somebody who doesn't have the authority to say "yes." In other words, go higher!

God is the highest you can go, and so when His Son told Peter to come out on the water, Peter had faith in His authority and ability. And Peter did the impossible. Jesus wasn't doing it for him. He was doing it himself, using his own faith in Jesus' words. A focused faith gives us the ability to access what we normally can't access in the natural—it moves not only us, but also the world around us. The water supported Peter because the water was designed by God to obey the laws of faith. The water stopped supporting him when his attention moved to it because even the water knows it's not God!

Doubt subtracts joy—again, the moment Peter doubted was the moment he started sinking and, buddy, there is no joy at all in falling in life! Nobody likes it. Can you imagine the glee Peter must have felt walking on the water? His whole life as a fishermen told him it was impossible, and yet he was doing the impossible. Imagine if it were you! I'd have been running around on that water; I think I might have wanted to dance a little, I don't know. All that joy immediately began to dissolve into thin air when the doubts in his mind started coming.

You've got to be a devout dissolver of doubt if you want joy as a believer. The faith life is about being focused on what God said. In our life, there are many "walking on the water" situations that require us to keep our eyes fixed on Christ. Living by faith is fun—it's a wide-open adventure—and it's in His presence that we find fullness of joy. We keep ourselves in His presence by keeping our heart pure and our eyes fixed on Him, and that's especially important when we're believing for what seems impossible.

Doubt will tell you things like, "You know cancer runs in your family." It'll tell you things like, "Your family is filled with a bunch of diabetics, so you're bound to get it, too." Doubt will say, "You know, crippling arthritis is just in your genes, you may as well accept it." Again, doubt just multiplies fear, divides attention, and subtracts joy.

It's hard to be joyful when you're full of fear. It's hard to think straight when you're flip-flopping between looking at Jesus and looking at the "waves" in your life.

So, you might as well just determine to keep your eyes on Jesus and believe, knowing that with Him, *all* things are possible. And, if by some chance your eyes wander to the waves in the middle and you *start* to sink as a result, He's **right there** to catch you. All you have to do is look right back to Him. The mercy of the Lord endures forever, and His mercy is always focused right on you. Jesus loves you. Don't ever forget it.

The Path of Obedience and the Contrary Winds

I'VE GOT TWO FEET ON THE WATER AND BOTH EYES ON THE SKY!

Peter was a tough man. He could pray for you one minute and cut your ear off the next. He was not a timid man. Jesus chose this man to lead for a reason—He not only had the faith few had, but he also had the guts to take risks others weren't willing to take. He would come to deny Jesus at one point but quickly ask for forgiveness and move on, which was something Judas couldn't do.

Peter learned to take control of his mind and accept Jesus' love, knowing that it was better to forgive himself and live to lead for Christ than to keep beating himself up with guilt and shame—he knew that if he wallowed in his own failings, he'd render himself useless to anybody. The work Jesus started was too important to Peter for him to let even *himself* get in the way. Peter was also quick to move. Peter *volunteered* to get out of the boat!

It Only Took One Word for Peter to Jump— Jesus said, "Come," and That Was Enough

Peter took it upon himself to stretch his faith. He wanted it to be personal. He wasn't content in the boat of religion waiting on Jesus to come—Peter saw Jesus and was so eager to be with Him, he voluntarily got out and met Jesus on the water. In the Old Testament, Moses waited on God. He didn't approach the cloud until God said,

"Come hither, come into the cloud, into the darkness," so to speak . . . but Peter was *not* like Moses. Peter wanted to jump!

Peter asked, and Jesus answered one little word: *"Come."* God progressively calls bolder and bolder people as time moves forward, and I believe in this fourth watch season that we aren't even going to need big words from God to move forward. Like Peter, we are going to see believers who look at the winds of change around the world and are willing to move out in faith, quickly and without need of convincing. Some may even ask God for more of what will only take faith to do, and like Peter, I believe many will hear Him say *"Come"* too.

I love the Gospels because they each give you different insights of how the events happened, according to the view of the one writing the book—and one of them says that after Peter walked, the boat was immediately put to shore. So, if you think about it, that means Jesus never did get into that boat. He began on the water, moved the boat to shore, and ended on the shore with Peter walking right from the water to land. Talk about a miracle!

One little word, *"Come"*—how many words from Christ does it take you to obey? How many scriptures do you have to read about healing to know Jesus heals? How many do you have to know to believe? How much struggle do you have to endure before you just believe that God wishes above all things that you prosper and be in health, even as your soul prospers? How many verses do you need before you will believe that God cares about the desires of your heart? How many before you believe that He is a "more than enough" God Who can be more than enough for you, too? Many believers are uncomfortable with blessings because lack is in them, when God wants limitlessness to be in them instead. Faith is about taking off the limits. It's about getting out of the boat of religion and going out onto the water with Jesus.

Peter may have been brash, but Paul the apostle was like a former ISIS leader—this was a bloodthirsty persecutor of Christians who thought he was doing great things when he was killing for a cause. Paul was called "Saul of Tarsus" before God intervened. He was not just a killer, but he was an elite academic, too. So, he had both great intelligence and ruthlessness. This was a man who was quick to obey the law and quick to enforce it, too—but while he was quick to obey others, God had to first smack him off a donkey on the road to Damascus to get him to change his killing ways.

I love how Paul responded to the smack. He immediately got a revelation: *"Lord, what wilt thou have me to do?"* (Acts 9:6). That cracks me up. You better know you're going to obey when the divine reaches out of Heaven to slap you. But I love that Paul didn't let grass grow under his feet either when he heard from God. Both Peter and Paul were quick to obey—a key element in the success of their faith in God.

The closer we get to Jesus' return in this fourth watch, the more we're going to have to be quick to obey. The beginning of Jesus' ministry was marked by a lot of persecution, and the people in that time needed to not just rely on their faith to hide, but also to use their faith with simple boldness to move forward and see God's plan come to fruition. The same will likely be required of us in the fourth watch.

We Must Be Prepared to Leave What Is Comfortable and Face the Unknown with Christ

The boat can symbolize many things, including whatever it is you're holding onto in life as security. The boat may be rocking hard and you may think it's saving your life—but all the boat has to do is go too far to the left or right and it may capsize, taking you down with it. Jobs. Businesses. Relationships. Whatever.

Your faith can't be in the "boat." It must be in the Lord. You're safer on the water with Jesus than you are hanging onto a boat for dear life without Him. I want you to see from Peter's story that Jesus didn't just save Peter from sinking and drowning, but He saved the boat, too.

When Jesus calmed the winds and the waves, the boat got the benefit just like the people got the benefit. The fishes and the loaves that were multiplied weren't left on the ground for people to stomp into the grass, but they were gathered as precious and saved at the word of Jesus Christ. Think about that.

Christ cares. He doesn't just care about saving you as a person but also saving whatever Satan has come to steal, kill, or destroy in your life. Jesus was abundant toward His people on the earth, and He is still abundant in Heaven. When will we have the faith to believe this? When will we get the religiosity out of our heart? It's time to make room in our hearts for what the early disciples had—great faith and boldness, quick obedience, and grace to do whatever the Lord asks us to do. We must be prepared to leave what is comfortable and face the unknown with Christ.

The Path of Obedience Always Has Contrary Winds

The winds of change today are contrary, make no mistake—but that's when impossible things happen, and that's when obedience is more critical than ever. Are you prepared? If you're struggling in your mind and heart, you haven't prepared. The power is on the water with Jesus. The peace is on the water with Jesus. The winds of change cease to matter when you are on the water and you're looking at Jesus.

"But why are the winds blowing?" you may ask. "Why" is a question people always ask, as if it matters in the end—"why" doesn't change anything for the better, "why" doesn't do anything but keep the pause in place between faith and manifestation of change. "Why" keeps you stuck in the boat with wind blowing and waves hitting you. It's fairly simple—the answer to "why" has a name, and it's Satan, who the Word calls the "prince of the power of the air." He works in the atmosphere—the air around you, the parallel world you can't see but most assuredly exists.

The will of God is the first two chapters of Genesis and the last two chapters of Revelation. In between those are 1,185 chapters of stealing, killing, and destroying by an archenemy of God named Satan. When it's all said and done, we're getting a new heaven and earth, and we will go back to the way it was supposed to be, and man will walk in the cool of the day with God again. But right now? We're in the messy middle! We're dealing with powers and principalities that work through human personalities, too—sin is saturated into the planet at the will of man. We fight against that by pushing the light. It's the only thing that works, and that's why just bemoaning the wind and waves doesn't work—it's why asking "why" doesn't help. "Why" has no power. Jesus has power. You have His name and He has given you authority to rebuke the wind and the waves, like He did with three faith-filled words: *"Peace be still!"*

You speak the Word and call those things that be not as though they were, until they are—by faith you are with Jesus right this second, right now. In whatever your situation, faith is the water. Doubt is the "why" and the whining! All you need is a little faith to see things shift. The path of obedience always has contrary winds—for you to know where your faith is, you must confront some wind and waves in life. It is better to obey than to sacrifice. All Peter had to do was *"Come"*—a small obedience in exchange for a miracle.

The Wind Pulls on the Weak Spots:
The Panickers, The Deniers, and The Realists

If anything is going to show you where the weak spots are in your faith and where you've learned to doubt, it's the waves and the wind of change. When the seas of life are roaring, I've noticed a few key ways people react.

The Panickers overreact the moment the boat starts rocking, even when there aren't a lot of wind or waves at all—they think they are sinking every time they move a little, but they aren't. They live in a state of worry, fear, and anxiety about what could happen if anything got worse—and if they see Jesus on the water, they immediately look back at the boat and hope the boat will save them because they can't keep their eyes on Jesus. Their fear actually brings them more of the same problems, over and over. They are calling it in with the words of their mouth and the thoughts they allow on repeat. They've learned to doubt so long that they think it's who they are . . . even though it most certainly isn't.

The Deniers feel the boat rock and pretend they're OK— they're sinking but singing, as if optimism alone will save them. The wind and waves can rock them so hard they're almost capsized, but they still won't obey God in any way shape or form. They're sinking but don't know it. They fool themselves and cry, but only in self-pity. They don't see the Power that's right in front of them. They don't believe it, really, in their heart. And they only start really regretting that choice when they are at death's door, overboard entirely. They've learned to doubt so long that they have never bothered to learn another way. They were too busy with other things in their boat to ever pay much attention to Jesus.

The Realists see the wind and waves very clearly, and they know the chaos is smacking them in the face—they feel every blow and know it's taking all they've got, but they still can't seem to look at Jesus. They're scared to look. They know what they've done. They've been living apart from Him for so long, their guilt holds them to the wooden boat that's threatening their life, and still they clench to the boat—white knuckling it out of some misplaced sense of shame. "Why would Jesus help me? I've turned away. I can't go back now. What will He think? I'm going to take my lumps because I deserve it anyway." They are miserable to the bone, crying the whole way down, not accepting that Jesus would never turn them away no matter what they've done or how long they've been gone. They've doubted themselves so long, they've got their doubt mixed up with God Himself.

Courage is realizing that only Jesus can save you from yourself—whether you panic, deny, or think you know it all and deserve what you get no matter how you react, Jesus is the answer, and He's on the water. And if you cling to the boat or your own ideas about the boat, you'll miss the opportunity that only faith can provide. It's an adventure in self-discovery, and sometimes that's the miracle you need most—because out of that comes the eye-opening revelation that there's more to life than just riding out the waves.

Two Feet on the Water and Both Eyes on the Sky

People make the wind and waves holy. People make the mountains in their way holy. People make the fig trees that don't produce fruit holy. They canonize whatever their doubt tells them is worth canonizing, and most of it is just out of the bad habit of learning to doubt over and over again.

Jesus doesn't promote doubt because He's not interested in making the difficult things of life just "part of it"—He will help you to push the light and overcome if you will let Him into your life enough to move at His Word. You'll be able to overcome senseless losses and react and respond in ways nobody can understand, but you know are right, if you will let Him.

Jesus will calm the waves and wind if you'll believe in His power more than the boat's false safety and speak His Words of peace in faith. He'll move the mountains if you use His Word and ways. You'll see the unproductive things that don't serve you dry up at the root, just like that fig tree, if you direct your words in faith and tell them to go.

Whether it's spiritual, physical, financial, or in any other area that you see rocked by the wind and waves of life, the Word of God and the relationship you have with Jesus can help you not just survive but thrive on the other side of the problem. In the story of Peter, the water-walking disciple, Jesus was on the water headed his way—He was coming to save, even in His own time of loss.

Today, I believe that Jesus sees all that is going on in the world, and He hurts because of what man has done to man . . . but like Peter looking out of the boat, I see that He is walking toward us. He's accessible to us by faith now, but soon and very soon, we are going to *see* the King! Some don't believe that Jesus is coming back, but for those of us who do? Well, we've got two feet on the water and both eyes on the sky! It's the fourth watch and everywhere we look, whether it's with the eyes of faith or the eyes in our head, we know that no matter what, Jesus is coming!

What Would Happen If You Decided to Never "Learn" to Doubt God Again?

As a born-again believer, you are very *noticeable* in the spirit realm. You're covered with a shaft of light that is the glory of God, and even the angels see it. When you speak the Word, they listen—not to just your words but to your *faith* in those words. The anointing reverberates when faith is applied to God's Word, creating a different atmosphere that makes receiving from God much easier.

Doubt is an enemy of spiritual change. Faith moves things in the spiritual atmosphere that you can't see—and it all starts with what you believe and what you say. God is waiting and listening, and His angels are, too. They are waiting on your words.

Who and what we identify with matters, and as believers, our identity should be firmly in Christ and firmly in faith. When you are living free in Christ, you are most like yourself and quick to let your faith rise to meet challenges. You don't conform to the way the world wants you to be; you're just yourself, living as God made you—free in Him without fear of man or fear of the devil.

Your faith rises easy. The Word rolls off your tongue easily. You've got it "in" you, and so when the waves kick up, that's what spills out—the Word, hope, and faith that Jesus is with you. And because of that, nothing can stop you from seeing good on the other side of the waves. You speak the Word and the spiritual atmosphere around you shifts. You speak the Word and the wheels of faith begin moving, bringing the manifestation of what you're believing for to pass.

You're the kind of believer that believes . . . for real. You're the kind that demons hate and angels protect—the kind that does right when you see it, goes out of your way to push the light, and enjoys life in the process . . . a fearless child of the One True God.

Can you see yourself in those words? What will you become from here on out? Will you become more of who you really are or will you choose what the world wants you to be? Where will you go from here? God's way or the other way? It's up to you. What you think and believe, you will become. Your life will go in the direction of your heart, even if your heart is not on your side. I believe that after this book, you'll have some new insights, some new ways of working out your own salvation with fear and trembling—which means with respect and awe of God, and His ways of saving you, even from yourself.

Doubt is an inside game. It's in your head and not anybody else's. Don't let the conditioning of your past determine your future. Don't let the fear of the winds of change keep you stuck. Faith is something you walk, not just talk. It's the forging of a new identity in Christ, and a force that you use every day if you want to live a life of never learning to doubt.

Getting What You Want, Getting Rid of What You Don't

You can manifest what you are believing for. You can get rid of what you don't want, too. This moving of things both toward and away happened instantly in the life of Christ all the time—healings came fast, coins in the fish's mouth came fast, and whatever He set His hand to do was done.

A lot of people only quote the "say to the mountain" scripture to teach faith, but I want you to remember that the mountain-moving faith teaching Jesus gave us began with a cursed fig tree. Jesus was getting rid of what He *didn't* want, and then teaching us how to do the same. Just like He calmed the wind and waves that nobody wanted, He wasn't just about bringing healing but about getting rid of problem-situations, too.

Matthew 21:19-22 says, *"And when He saw a fig tree in the way, He came to it, and found nothing thereon, but leaves only, and said unto it, Let no fruit grow on thee henceforward for ever. And presently the fig tree withered away. And when the disciples saw it, they marvelled, saying, How soon is the fig tree withered away! Jesus answered and said unto them, Verily I say unto you, If ye have faith, and doubt not, ye shall not only do this which is done to the fig tree, but also if ye shall say unto this mountain, Be thou removed, and be thou cast into the sea; it shall be done. And all things, whatsoever ye shall ask in prayer, believing, ye shall receive."*

Speaking what you want and don't want by faith to the actual "thing" and *believing* at the time that you pray is what He taught—and receiving is the consequence of doing those things. I've written on this in detail in other books, so I won't go into this here, but I want you to see that you don't really talk to God about the problem as much as you talk directly to the problem.

Your faith is in Jesus, but your problem needs to hear your voice. Words are important. They are vessels that contain your future. Your future is literally quite often in your own mouth. It's in your heart, too. Out of the abundance of the heart, the mouth will speak! It's how we're made. It's what we do. Now, we just have to live like Jesus and *not* doubt the Father, as well as *not* doubt ourselves!

Jesus is our guide—and there is no better example of faith being used to manifest what we want than His example. What did He do? Here are just a few things: Jesus *prayed* alone, often in the wilderness—He did not forsake alone-time with God, and thought it was so important that He even put off things religious people would have thought were more important. Jesus *fasted*—He put His flesh in check bodily in order to tune into the Spirit more effectively, and because He put His Spirit *first*, He could even conquer the temptations of the devil at his weakest physical point.

Jesus read the Word until it was like breathing, being instant in season and out—He could quote it and teach it like no one who has ever lived, but, most importantly, He *believed* it and *acted* on it. There is no greater "doer of the Word" than Jesus Christ, and the Word is filled with stories of His miracles of healing and provision. Yet, Jesus told us that *we* would go on to do the works He did, and greater (John 14:12). How? We can only do the works He did, and greater, *one* way—by never learning to doubt that we can.

If You Want to Move the Mountain, Don't Focus on the Desert

Jesus went to weddings and parties. He had fun. He was not a killjoy stick-in-the-mud who lived at church and hid away from people. Jesus was in the muck and mud with sinners just as much as He was in the synagogue with the religious rulers of the day. Jesus was a Man for all people because He is a God for all people. Jesus didn't care if you were a woman, a man, a certain color, or from a culture different than His own. He saw us all as equally loved in the sight of God—in Christ, there is no male or female, Jew or Greek, neither bond nor free. Under God, we are all precious and worthy no matter who we are or where we come from . . . and especially no matter what anyone else has told us.

Jesus hated sickness and disease. He healed everywhere that the people's faith would allow. Jesus wept at the loss of His friend, even though He knew He was going to raise the man from the dead—He is touched by our feelings, and He is near to the brokenhearted. He's not above crying with us, but He wants us instead to dry our eyes and have faith in Him to change the situations that bring us pain. This is what Jesus is all about.

You know, Jesus couldn't go to funerals—He'd mess them up. He didn't care if you already bought the tomb! He was compassionate but strong. He didn't like the religious hierarchy putting so much pressure on the people. He refused rules that only served to make the life of people more difficult, and at the same time He preached it was good to pay your taxes!

Jesus stood up for truth and was willing to take the heat for what He believed. He was a status-quo-breaking Rabbi who blew the establishment away at just twelve years old. Today, we are still unraveling the profound truth of His teachings, and we likely will for all of eternity. In Heaven, we'll gain so many new truths! Can you imagine?

Jesus was a great storyteller. He chose to use parables more than any other way to communicate deep truths. Jesus knew that we love stories, and that we are motivated to change if we feel emotionally connected—and so His stories were good ones. He has more to tell. You'll have to get to Heaven to hear them . . . so make sure you go! You can't ever get far enough away that you can't turn back. You can't ever do anything bad enough to make Him say, "Naaa, I'm not forgiving that one." No, Jesus always meets people where they are, no matter what they've done, and He can help anybody to change—and create a new story worth living and telling.

As believers, after salvation, I think the moment we realize that we *can* have what we say, we should start saying what we want in faith—saying what our heart truly desires and stop playing around with what we *don't* want. If you want a mountain in your life to move, don't focus on and talk about the desert. If you want something, say it—don't waste your breath on what you *aren't* interested in and *don't* want.

Faith makes complaining a waste of energy. Jesus said what He wanted, and so should you. Believe when you pray that you've already got it and that it's a done deal. *"Now faith is the substance of things hoped for, the evidence of things not seen"* from Hebrews 11:1 starts with *"Now faith is"*—it's not a question, "Is faith now?" Put your faith in the now all the time.

Stop talking about what you want like it's way off in the future. The sooner you see it in the now, the quicker it'll get done. The more you keep putting it in the future with your words, the more it stays in "far off someday." If you want to manifest right away, stop even thinking about "someday." Now. Faith. Is.

Don't say, "I'll try" when it comes to faith. Trying doesn't get much done. If you invite somebody to church and they say, "I'll try to make it," what happens? They usually don't show up. You've got to show up for yourself to see God's plan come to pass in your life. I've seen miracles in my own life that I know would not have happened if I listened to people or even my own mind that tried to tell me, "You can't" or "You'll never." Choosing not to doubt God has given me a free heart and an imaginative mind.

I don't care if people call me a dreamer, because they're partially right—I'm a dreamer, I'm a hearer and I'm a doer, too. And that's why I have so many testimonies to tell! God has been good to me. I speak well of myself to myself. I know who I am, and I know

Who is on my side. I refuse to doubt God because that's going against God, and I refuse to doubt my ability to believe because that's going against me! The devil fights enough; I don't see any good reason in fighting myself. Do you?

If You Can't Recognize Yourself, Doubting Has Likely Become a Habit

So, I identify with healing. I identify with prosperity. I identify with forgiveness, too. What you identify with matters because you act accordingly. It shows up in your daily life. Have you ever deserved judgment but received mercy? Not just from God, but from people? It happened to me recently just going to the mall.

I was driving, and there was a "do not turn" sign I didn't notice. The light turned green, I turned, and sure enough . . . a cop was there! I saw his lights and heard his *boop-boop* sounding siren, and I immediately pulled over. I wasn't even worried about it though. I told Cathy, "I must have done something wrong. Let's see."

So, the policemen gets out of his car, comes to mine, and says, "You're trying to make the light, aren't you?"

I said, "No, sir."

He said, "Yes, you were. Do you know that you just went through where only emergency vehicles should go through?"

"I didn't see the sign," I said, "but I apologize, I made a mistake. You write me a ticket. I deserve it."

He just looked at me. I guess he doesn't hear "I deserve it" much!

"Give me your license and registration," he said, and I started looking everywhere. I was driving Cathy's car and not my truck, and as I'm looking, he says, "I'll be back" and goes to his car.

He comes back and says, "I'm not going to give you a ticket."

"No, give me one," I say, "I deserve it. I did this, I know. Sir, I apologize."

He looked at me as if to say *shut up and just get out of here*, but then he just looked at me and said, "You shocked me so bad, you told the truth . . . I've been listening to lies all day long." I was shocked too, suddenly, just hearing that. I told him my wife and I were going to eat dinner, and he said to have a nice one but to not make that wrong turn again. I said, "I promise I won't" and drove off thinking about how much lying we encounter every day, especially the police.

The bottom line though is this: it's our job as believers to be truth-speakers and especially if we do wrong—that's the believer's way. We should shock people with our ability to be vulnerable enough to speak the truth. We should shock them with our faith and our good deeds. We should shock them with our ability to say, "I was wrong" if we were wrong. We don't have to apologize for what we didn't do, but we should speak truthfully every chance we get—and even more so when we don't do the right thing. We're called to be lights in the darkness, and to push the light every chance we get.

Why could I so easily tell that policemen the truth? I believe it's because I recognize who I am in Christ—my identity is never in my mistakes. My identity is in Christ and in the truth. Never learning to doubt God is about identifying more with what He says we can be than with any human failing. We all fall short, but He is the forgiver and the lifter of our head—He's the One Who helps us turn it around.

I don't know about you, but I want to be on the side of truth and good. If I mess up, I want to be the one who says, "I messed up!" I'm willing to take the consequences, but it's amazing, though, how often mercy comes instead—I believe it's because what you sow, that you'll reap. I've sown a lot of mercy along the way in my life. So, I've got harvests of it in waiting—and they are harvests I hope I never have to use! My goal is not to fall short but to aim to do right as much as I can and as best as I can.

Some people think it's about humility to fess up to wrong; I think it's just about being truthful. If the Word tells us to obey the laws of the land, then we should do it, whether it's big or small in our own eyes. If the Word tells us to be honorable people who speak the truth and not a bunch of lies, then we should speak the truth. If you say you tell the truth but don't—that's a "hearer only" thing you need to work on, starting now. Your identity needs to be firmly in the "doer" and the "do right" category. You need to see yourself as active and honorable, and merciful, too.

If you can't recognize yourself in what the Word says, then doubting has likely become your habit. Just determine to stop. Today. Now. Then, make a commitment to start practicing. You are who God says you are. When situations come up where you could criticize yourself or do the wrong thing, if you can at all help it, don't do either! Remember your identity is in Christ—remember who you are and act from *that* place. That's the real you, without temptation to be otherwise. Choose it. Make it a habit to be who you are in Christ, to walk in the light of God's view of you and push the light.

Don't Pause, Don't Hesitate and Don't Miss Out— Today Is the Day, and Daylight Is Burning!

If you have the power to give mercy to someone who does wrong, show mercy. If someone wants to show mercy to you, then take it. If you see someone do wrong, help them. Remind yourself that "Do unto others as you'd have them do unto you" is at its most "golden" when forgiveness is what's at work and when mercy is what is being applied.

When Jesus was on the cross and prayed, *"Father, forgive them; for they know not what they do,"* He wasn't just talking about the men who crucified Him that day—He was talking about every single misguided and blind-to-the-truth person who goes against the laws of God.

It's not enough to just read the Word; we must do it. And it's not enough to just do it; we must identify with it so much that we see its truth as who we *are.* God's Word is not something we read, it's part of who we are—it's how we live because we're God's children.

God is love, so let's be love. God is patient, so let's be patient, too. God is wise and truthful, so let us be wise and truthful in this dark world, too. Can you imagine what this world would be like if we all believed God's words and lived it—what would it be like if we not only believed in ourselves but also treated others the way we want to be treated? What would it look like to see billions of people find out who they are in Christ and never learn to doubt? What a wonderful world it'd be!

The hesitation to believe that God is a good Father Who has our best interests at heart makes us pause in our faith—it makes us pause in believing in His love for us and in doing all the wonderful things we were created to do. Faith works by love; we must get His love for us down deep! We're meant to be doers who work in love. In the "pausing" of doubt, we miss out—we lose the ambition to take actions that would shift our life. Missed options for greatness in our own lives. Missed opportunities to be doers of good in a dark world.

What if you decided that you just don't want to doubt God or yourself anymore? What if every other believer decided the same thing . . . and the whole of us as the body of Christ chose to simply *believe* and move in our God-given freedom? What would the world look like if we simply believed that we *are* who God said we are? What if we believed we could have what God said we could have? What if no matter who or what rose up against us—even the devil himself—we just laughed, were of good cheer, and ready to win, knowing that if God be for us, who really can be against us? And what if we didn't just believe it, but we *acted* on it? Guess what? We can. We really can!

Today's the day, man . . . and daylight is burning! *I* have another shot at never learning to doubt today. *You* have another shot at never learning to doubt today, too. Will you take it? After this whole book, I sure hope you take it!

Faith Is Our Heritage, Our Identity, and Our Legacy— Thank You for Being with Me Through These Pages

Thanks for reading and letting me share some of what I know with you. I appreciate you being with me through these many pages, and I hope you'll take some of these teachings and apply them to your daily life. Most of all, I pray to God that you take the challenge of faith and decide to never "learn" to doubt—that you put the doubt junk behind you once and for all, because I know without a shadow of doubt that you *can* do it.

Look, if *I* can have faith and refuse doubt every day, you can, too! We have the same Father God. The very same Jesus has saved us, and the same Holy Spirit that's living inside of me is living inside of you, too. We're family! We're the family of God, we're siblings in the faith, and we have access to the same spiritually-inherited good traits that Jesus had.

Faith is our heritage as well as our identity and our legacy! We are not doubters; we're *believers*. I'm convinced that, moment by moment and choice by choice, we can live in pure, wondrous, and childlike faith . . . never learning to doubt *all* the days of our life. Are you with me?

Until Jesus comes back to get us and we meet in the clouds, or until I see you in Heaven one day, I pray God's Spirit and His Word will be your guide every day. May you live free, healed, whole, blessed, and joyful—*always* living by faith and *never* learning to doubt!

Jesse Duplantis

J esus is called so many names, but one of my favorites is "The Good Shepherd"—the One Who would leave everything to go and find that one lost sheep. If you don't know Jesus or if you just aren't where you should be and want to come back home to God, would you take a moment to pray this prayer?

All you have to do is reach out to God with a sincere heart, and He will reach right back down to you and help you right where you are. Accepting Christ changes everything because it changes the heart— it opens the door for a new life in Christ, where all the old things are passed away and everything becomes new. He's listening, and He loves you. No matter what you've done or how far you've gone, He has made it easy to turn around and just come back where you need to be. Home. Are you ready? This prayer is just a guide, and I encourage you to pray from your heart. Remember, you are a spirit, and God is going to recreate you from the inside out. That's how He works. It starts in the heart. Would you pray this prayer with me now?

"Lord Jesus, I know You hear me, and I want You to know that I need You in my life. Thank You for coming for me, for loving me, and for taking me just as I am. I believe You are the Son of God and that You came to save everyone, including me. I ask You to forgive me and help me from the inside out right now—I know You see my spirit and You know my heart, and I accept Your love and sacrifice for me. Thank You for saving me and for bringing me back where I should be, which is with You. I accept You now as my Lord and Savior. I am Yours and You are now mine, and I will never live without You again. I release all my shame and guilt to You, Lord. I give everything I have in my heart over to You to make clean and pure before You. Be with me now, Lord. I accept by faith that from this day on, you will always be with me. On earth. In Heaven. For the rest of my days and all of eternity. Show me Your ways, Lord, and help me to grow and live with an open heart. Starting now, let me always be open to recognize and accept Your love and all Your many blessings. Help me to become the person You've created and always called me to be. Thank You, Lord! Amen."

If you prayed this prayer, I want to welcome you into the Family of God. I'm your brother now. And you've got brothers and sisters all over this world, and many generations back as well…but you'll meet them in Heaven later! God has so many good kids and some bad ones too, but they're all His kids, and He loves each one. Find a good church. Read your Bible and listen to messages that inspire you. Go and grow! Remember that God is good, the journey of life is so much better with Him, and your best days are always going to be when you allow His Spirit to lead you. Thank you for giving me the honor of sharing my thoughts and my heart with you through this book. God bless you on your journey!

J esse Duplantis, minister of the Gospel, motivational speaker, television personality, and best-selling author, has been in full-time ministry since 1978 and is the founder of Jesse Duplantis Ministries, located in the Greater New Orleans area of south Louisiana in the United States of America. With over four decades of sharing his unique blend of humor and faith around the world, generations of believers have been inspired by his messages and countless numbers have come to know Jesus Christ as Savior through his ministry.

Known for his unflinching, status-quo-breaking messages and humorous take on experiences in the life of the believer, Jesse continues to draw large audiences of believers through social media, television, and meetings held around the world. With speaking engagements booked years in advance, Jesse Duplantis continues to keep an intense traveling schedule, flying throughout the United States and the world preaching the Gospel of Jesus Christ. With no booking agents pursuing meetings for him and no set fees imposed upon churches for speaking engagements, Jesse chooses his outreach meetings based on the same two criteria he always has: invitations that come in and prayer over each one. This uncommon way of scheduling in today's world means Jesse's many followers may find him speaking in some of the largest churches and venues in America and the world, as well as a great many small and growing congregations, too. No church is too big or small for the Holy Spirit, as he says.

Side by side with his wife Cathy Duplantis, the co-founder and chief of staff of Jesse Duplantis Ministries and the senior pastor of Covenant Church in Destrehan, Louisiana, Jesse continues to fulfill his life's calling by daily taking up the Great Commission of Jesus Christ: *"Go ye into all the world, and preach the Gospel to every creature"* (Mark 16:15). Through social media, television broadcasts, books, and other ministry products, as well as through many evangelistic meetings, the JDM website, the JDM app, and *Voice of the Covenant* magazine, Jesse Duplantis continues to see growth in his ministry and expand each year while maintaining his roots. Jesus is the center of his life. The salvation of lost people and the growth of believers is the purpose of his ministry. And for both he and his wife, every day is another day to *"Reach People and Change Lives, One Soul at a Time."*

The Most Wonderful Time of the Year
Uncommon Lessons from the Christmas Story

Your Everything Is His Anything
Expand Your View of What Prayer and Faith Can Do

Advance in Life
From Revelation to Inspiration to Manifestation

The Big 12
My Personal Confidence-Building Principles for Achieving Total Success

Living at the Top
How to Prosper God's Way and Avoid the Pitfalls of Success

For by IT…FAITH
If You Don't Know What "IT" Is, You Won't Have It!

DISTORTION
The Vanity of Genetically Altered Christianity

The Everyday Visionary
Focus Your Thoughts, Change Your Life

What in Hell Do You Want?

Wanting a God You Can Talk To

Jambalaya for the Soul
Humorous Stories and Cajun Recipes from the Bayou

Breaking the Power of Natural Law
Finding Freedom in the Presence of God

God Is Not Enough, He's Too Much!
How God's Abundant Nature Can Revolutionize Your Life

Heaven: Close Encounters of the God Kind

The Ministry of Cheerfulness

OTHER CONTENT:

Other ministry resources by Jesse Duplantis are available through www.jdm.org, the JDM App, and Total.JDM.org.

To contact Jesse Duplantis Ministries with prayer requests, praise reports, or comments, or to schedule Jesse Duplantis at your church, conference, or seminar, please write, call, or email:

> Jesse Duplantis Ministries
> PO Box 1089
> Destrehan, LA 70047
> 985-764-2000
> www.jdm.org

We also invite you to connect with us on social media:

Facebook:	/JesseDuplantisMinistries
Twitter:	@jesse_duplantis
Instagram:	@jesseduplantisministries
YouTube:	/jesseduplantismin
Pinterest:	/JesseDuplantisMinistries

Made in the USA
Middletown, DE
11 November 2021